UNDERSTANDING HINDUISM

(Scriptures, Deities, Prayers, Mantras, Meditation Techniques, Yoga, Karma, Hindu Concept of Creation, Nature & Science)

UNDERSTANDING HINDUISM

(Scriptures, Deities, Prayers, Mantras, Meditation Techniques, Yoga, Karma, Hindu Concept of Creation, Nature & Science)

Kandiah Sivaloganathan

ZORBA BOOKS

ZORBA BOOKS

Publishing Services by Zorba Books, October 2020

Website: www.zorbabooks.com
Email: info@zorbabooks.com
Contact: 0124-4259579/8800509579

Cover design © Dhiraj

Print Book ISBN: 978-93-90011-55-1

Ebook ISBN: 978-93-90011-56-8

Zorba Books Pvt. Ltd. (opc)
Sushant Arcade,
Next to Courtyard Marriot,
Sushant Lok 1, Gurgaon – 122009, India

A Brief Introduction to the Ancient Religion of Hinduism

Dedicated

To

Bhagawan Sri Sathya Sai Baba

&

Saints

‘No religion on earth preaches the dignity of humanity in such a lofty strain as Hinduism.’

—Swami Vivekananda

PREFACE

In the modern world, dominated by science and technology, the concept of religion is disillusioning for many people. Today's youth, in particular, with their inquiring mind, find it difficult to believe in the idea of religion as they can't see any tangible benefit from following a specific faith. They seek empirical evidence about the existence of an ultimate power called God. Students are taught to question and make enquiries before they accept anything they do not understand. Therefore, students are unable to comprehend the idea of God, which they find difficult to grasp without significant evidence.

Increasingly, humans are becoming indifferent to the concept of Divinity or God as a result of the comforts and conveniences provided by the unprecedented development of science and technology. Therefore, humans are puzzled regarding the need for a Divine entity, God, for their day to day life.

Today, most of humanity attempts to understand anything related to life through the five senses. This is because the knowledge of all material things is gained through scientific investigations with the tools that enhance humans' sense organs, such as electrons microscopes, telescopes, etc. The use of this kind of technology is prevalent in high schools and universities to investigate the material aspects of the universe. Since no technology is taught in schools and universities to understand how life throbbing within them-namely body, mind, which includes thought and emotion, and energy functions. Students are, therefore, at a loss to understand how their physical, psychological and energy systems of the body function. Because of this type of education system, with emphasis on the understanding of the material aspect of the external world, only scientific methods used to understand the physical world are available to humans to explore and understand anything, including their own lives. This situation is not satisfactory and more need to be done to help humans to understand how their own body, mind and energy function.

Sages and seers, along with present-day seekers of Truth, experience God not through the five sensory organs but through their intuition or Consciousness. Without the first-hand experience of Divinity, it is difficult to fully understand the language of religions. Therefore, most humans base their faith in Divinity or God, believing the information provided by preachers and scripters.

Prophets in many religions, including enlightened ones like Buddha, Jesus Christ and Mohammad, have preached their own experience of their enlightenment, their vision, in the language of their time. The language is not precise and fails to provide the real experience of the prophets. This type of preaching is similar to a situation where one attempts to describe the smell of a flower to another person who has never smelt the particular flower before. In order to experience the scent of a flower, one needs to smell the flower themselves. It is not enough to listen to another person's description, which will not provide the real experience of smelling a flower.

The scriptures, which were written in the language of that time, require interpretation in present-day language to understand the meaning they attempt to convey. The meaning that is conveyed also depends on the eloquence of the interpreter. Also, preaching based on one person's interpretation can cause confusion or misunderstanding among the followers of that particular religion.

Although scriptures provide guidance for attaining enlightenment and experience of the Divine, this guidance is often not highlighted by religious institutions, perhaps due to a lack of sufficient people who have had direct experience of the Divine, that is to say, enlightened persons. Therefore, the preaching is mainly concerned with the glory of God, along with the social and moral code one should follow to go to heaven.

Religious scholars, in their talks, also amplify the prophets' teachings and even go a bit further by attempting to emphasise that their way is the best path not only for their followers but also for all humanity to reach heaven or God. Although, preaching in this manner is done with the best of intentions, it immediately sets up a fence around each religion and creates conflict between them regarding the best path to follow. Religious conflict of this nature has even resulted in a number of wars, including the present conflicts in the Middle East. It is, therefore, understandable why today's youth is indifferent to religious teachings.

Most of the younger generations get a very brief understanding of their religion. They experience religion simply by observing the religious practices of their parents, relatives and friends. The spiritual knowledge they gather from their surroundings is amplified if they attend churches or temples. In some cases, even such experiences don't exist due to their family's apathy towards religion. In school, too, there's no introduction to religion, particularly in state schools where students are from different backgrounds, so as not to offend any particular community.

Unlike in the past, very few, including parents, have the time or take the time, to read religious texts to understand their faith. Lack of knowledge of the sacred texts is particularly high in Hinduism, which does not have a holy book, unlike the Bible for Christians or the Quran for Muslims.

Hindu scriptures, from the Vedas, are without beginning and end as these are an accumulation of the treasures of spiritual laws discovered at different times. Spiritual law is the relationship between individual spirits and the soul, and these laws existed even before they were discovered and will continue to function after we have forgotten them. The spiritual laws are just like the law of gravity that existed before it was discovered and still continues to exist.

In order to understand Hinduism, one needs to study the various scriptures like the *Vedas*, *Upanishads*, *Mahabharata*, and the *Ramayana*, among others. The *Agamas* are also important theological texts and practical manuals, which govern many of the current practices prevalent in Hinduism.

In the Hindu tradition, there is no word that explicitly refers to a supreme being, such as the English word God. In Hinduism, self-realisation is what Hindus are seeking. In essence, this is a path through which one is able to merge with the omnipresent Creator, the Divinity within all. Therefore, I have tried not to use the word God in this edition of the book as far as possible.

Some Hindus consider the *Bhagavad Gita*, a part of the *Mahabharata,* the great epic, as equivalent to the Bible. The *Bhagavad Gita* is a dialogue that took place between Lord Krishna and the Pandava prince, Arjuna, on the battle field of Kurukshetra where the battle between the Pandavas and Kauravas took place.

In this day and age, it is a big undertaking for busy individuals to read and understand these scriptures. This book is an effort to provide a very brief background and introduction to Hinduism, along with some simple daily religious rituals of a Hindu householder. I hope this will kindle interest in the readers and encourage them to read some of the scriptures and refine their knowledge of Hinduism.

Practising some of the spiritual practices provided in Hindu scriptures are useful tools for daily practice. These practices can bring health and wellbeing in our hectic lives.

I have revised the original version of the book, *A Brief Introduction to Hinduism*, to explain and amplify ideas that required clarification.

I render my grateful thanks to my friend, Paul Ward–Harvey BA, LLM, for meticulously editing the first manuscript. I also thank my son, Lavan, for formatting and proofreading the text of the first manuscript.

Kandiah Sivaloganathan
Sydney, Australia August 2020

CONTENT

1

ORIGIN OF THE WORD HINDUISM

The word 'Hindu' is derived from the Sanskrit word 'Sindhu', which is the local name for the river Indus that flows through the Himalayas in the North-Western part of India. Sindhu also means sea. In ancient Indian culture, the ocean surrounding India was known as Sindhu Mahasagara. The Greeks used the word Hindu or Indu to refer to the country and the people who occupied the land from the Indus river to the Sindhu Mahasagara. The people who occupied the land from the Himalayas to the Sindhu Mahasagara were known as Hindus to the foreigners. From the 16th century, residents of India also began referring to themselves as Hindus to distinguish themselves from other nationalities such as Greeks, Persians, and Turks.

The subcontinent of India was, and continues to be, a land of tapestries of culture. It encompasses breathtaking complexity of diversity. There are over 200 different languages and a variety of spiritual practices. Despite all these differences, outsiders who came to India referred to the people of India as one unit and called them Hindus.

The local citizens of India did not refer to their spiritual practices by any particular name. Ancient Vedic scriptures formed the basis of the spiritual practices in India, although with different practices, to suit the language and culture of the locality. Thousands of years ago, without speedy transport and communication, one could not expect the practices of one part of the continent to be conveyed to another area, hundreds of miles away. Thus, the customs and spiritual practices developed in India independently and remain without uniformity even today.

The people of the Indian subcontinent did not refer to their spiritual practices as a particular religion, but they referred to people as devotees of the specific deities they worshipped. This concept did not prevent Hindus from worshipping other deities. Many Hindus worshipped all deities according to their needs and to suit auspicious occasions.

The word 'religion' was not part of ancient Indian culture. The idea of organised religion is an import from the West. The word 'Hinduism' was introduced to reflect certain spiritual practises in the late 19th century with the publication of the book *Hinduism* (1877), written by Sir Monier – Williams, the notable Oxford scholar and author of the *Monier-Williams Sanskrit dictionary*. The word 'Hinduism', therefore, originated from outside India, building on the centuries-old usage of the word 'Hindu'. Indians have rejected the term Hinduism in different ways, but the usage has persisted. The word 'Hinduism' now refers to varied spiritual practices in India. Some Indians preferred to refer to their spiritual practice as the 'Vedic Lifestyle', relating to the ancient spiritual texts known as the Vedas. Others referred to these practices as Sanatana Dharma (eternal law). Over time, the majority of Hindus, as a result of colonisation, have accepted the term 'Hinduism' to refer to their spiritual practices.

2

BASIC SCRIPTURES

Hinduism is one of the oldest religions in the world with around one billion followers. What sets Hinduism apart from other world religions is the fact that it has no single founder, no sole scripture, no common set of teachings. It does not espouse any one philosophical concept or one set of rituals. It does not satisfy any traditional practise of any religion. Therefore, many scholars refer to Hinduism as 'a way of life'. In a gist, Hinduism is a way of seeking the Truth by means of touching the spirit (Life) within you and how everything came to be.

Teachings in all Hindu scriptures focus on how to attain absolute independence or total freedom. This absolute freedom is referred to as Moksha in Hinduism, which is also known as Enlightenment. Attaining Moksha is what Hinduism is all about. This concept is what makes Hinduism different from other religions, which often talk about heaven and hell. In Hinduism, there is no such thing as eternal hell or eternal heaven.

Hinduism is also known as 'Sanatana Dharma' — the eternal way or the eternal order beyond human origins.

Although there is no single book that specifies the practice of Hinduism, several ancient scriptures provide the foundation for the practice of Hinduism. I have briefly outlined some of the primary spiritual texts and their teachings below:

2.1 The Vedas and the Upanishads

The Vedas and the Upanishads are broadly considered as the most important ancient Hindu scriptures. Vedas means knowledge. The Vedas are a large body of texts formulated by rishis, seers, saints and sages thousands of years ago in India. Over the years, this knowledge, made available by the rishis, concerning the Eternal Principles, was passed on from one generation to another through word of mouth and eventually made available in the written form. This written form of the knowledge of the Eternal Principles is known as *the Vedas*. The originally spoken literature is known as *Shruti* (heard). Shruti works are considered to be heard and transmitted by earthly sages. Shruti is considered more authoritative than the Vedic text. In the modern day, the Vedic text has more influence than Shruti. This is because when the Vedas are verbally recited, specific vibrations are produced that have certain required effects. This is lacking in the text version of the Vedas. Even today, specific mantras are chanted loudly to induce the required effects that chanting creates through these vibrations.

There are four main Vedas: Rig Veda, Sama Veda, Yajur Veda and Atharva Veda.

Rig Veda contains the hymns and songs of the rishis.

Sama Veda is a liturgical collection of the melodies for chanting and giving meaning to the words in the Rig Veda.

Yajur Veda is also a liturgical collection and meets the demands of the ceremonial religion.

Atharva Veda is different from the above three, and contains hymns that are more diverse and consists of spells and charms present at that time.

Several others cover other aspects of human endeavours, including the arts and sciences.

The Upanishads are a collection of texts that contain some of the underlying principles and central philosophical concepts of Hinduism. The teachings of the Upanishads revolve around the realisation of the ultimate Divine. This realisation is the same as realising our Self, the Atman, within us.

The term 'Upanishad' denotes the study and practice of the inner truth. '*Upa*' means the process of studying with '*Nishta*' or steadfastness; 'Shad' means the attainment of Ultimate Reality. The Upanishads describe the various stages of realisation of one's essential reality. They point out not only the duties and obligations one has to bear, but also the actions to be carried out and those to be avoided. The Upanishads are collectively called the *Vedanta*.

The Upanishads contain the noblest ideas and thoughts that hold good to this day. Several scientists and outstanding people, such as Erwin Schrodinger who was a 1933 Noble Prize winner in physics, deeply appreciated the noble thoughts in Upanishads. According to him, '*The multiplicity is only apparent. This is the doctrine of the Upanishads and not of the Upanishads only. The mystical experience of the union with God regularly leads to this view, unless strong prejudices stand in the way*'.

2.2 The *Agamas*

In addition to the *Vedas*, the *Agamas* are another type of ancient Hindu scriptures that govern the present-day practice of Hinduism. The *Agamas* literally mean traditions, 'that which comes down'. The *Agamas* provide practical and experimental concepts of Hindu religious beliefs and practices. These texts consist of three groups: Shaivism (related to Siva), Vaishnavism (associated with Vishnu) and Shaktism (related to Devi). The Indonesian Balinese Hindus have their own *Agamas* known as the *Agama Bali*.

The *Agamas* are more voluminous than the *Vedas*, but they are not known to most as they are written entirely in the Grantha script (Appendix A) and prevail mostly in southern India. The Grantha script is an old Tamil script. The Malayalam and Sinhala alphabets are the direct descendants of Grantha. Only a few *Agama* texts have been translated into English and French. The non-availability of *Agama* texts in English and other languages has led to the spread of distorted versions of Hinduism among westerners and modern Hindus. The Agama traditions comprise approximately two-third of the Hindu heritage.

The Hindu view typically presented is Vedic, and Sanskrit centred, which is not an accurate representation of the present-day practice of Hinduism. In the Vedic form of worship, with the fire ritual (*homa*), there is no physical representation of the deity, but where worship was necessary, visual fire represented Divinity, all deities. In the Agama rites, the deity is represented by some visible emblem in the form of a statue, picture or a lingam. The lingam is not a *murti,* but a sign, mark and emblem of the supreme.

HOMA

Today, Hinduism all over the world, and in particular in the subcontinent of India, is based on the *Agamas* and not the Vedic form as Swami Vivekananda has observed. The Agama scriptures cover cosmology, philosophical doctrines, meditation, yoga, mantras, temple construction, deity worship and worship in temples and homes, alter worship, temple ceremonies, and life-to-death sacraments. That is what Hinduism is all about. However, in today's practice of Hinduism, the *Vedas* provide the mantras, the literature (bhakti literature) and hymns to be sung in temples and homes.

The technical knowledge provided in the *Agamas* for temple construction and installation of deities is to establish a sanctified space for devotees to spend time in this space, in order to rejuvenate themselves. Therefore, it is vital for the devotees to spend some time quietly in the space of the temple to absorb this energy to rejuvenate themselves.

In the Vedic religion, the specialists are Brahmins, but in the *Agamas*, the specialists are referred to as 'Gurukal' or 'Diksha'. According to the *Agamas*, Gurukal or Diksha are open to all men and women, and there are no restrictions. The male assistants in the temples are called *pandarams,* and female assistants who prepare the lamps and wick, and carry them to the shrine, light them and pass them to the Gurukal are referred to as the 'slaves of Rudra'.

The core of Hinduism is in the *Agamas*, and the core of the *Agamas* is in the temples, and the core of temples is in the deities. The *Agamas* dictate all the rituals we see in the temples today.

2.3 The *Ramayana* and the *Mahabharata*

Following the *Upanishads* come the epics — the *Ramayana* and the *Mahabharata.* These two epics are a source of inspiration and direction to the Hindu way of life. In each epic, there are shorter stories, tales and discourses on subjects that pertain to the present-day life situations.

The *Ramayana* is not merely the story of Rama and Sita that took place during 7400 BC, it is a story that we live every moment of our lives. The epic narrates the story of Rama, the prince of Kosala; his banishment from the kingdom by his father, King Dasharatha; his travels across India with his wife, Sita, and brother, Lakshmana; the kidnapping of his wife by the demon king of Sri Lanka, Ravana, resulting in war and finally, the killing of Ravana and the return to Ayodhya with Sita to be crowned king. For Hindus, Lord Ram is an *avatar*. *Avatar* translates as 'descent' and refers to the appearance or reincarnation of God on earth, for the sake of his devotees, to restore order and morality.

In the *Ramayana,* there are shorter stories and tales, which are universal and guide us regarding how we should behave and conduct our lives in various circumstances. The *Ramayana* is still very relevant to present-day society, as the epic has valuable lessons to offer about all facets of civilisation, including areas as diverse as the art of governance. For example, it details the advanced political organisation that existed in Ayodhya to provide maximum happiness to maximum people for a maximum period based on the principle of Dharma. King Rama signalled man's ability to govern nations.

In the *Ramayana*, the prince Rama lifted the mighty bow of Siva in the court of Emperor Janaka, thus winning the hand of princess Sita, Janaka's adopted daughter. After some years, Rama's father, Emperor Dasaratha, decided to step down and crown Rama as the Emperor. Just hours before the auspicious ceremony, due to a promise he had made to one of his queens, Dasaratha exiled Rama to the forest for fourteen years. Rama happily accepted his father's orders and left for the forest with Sita, accompanied by his younger brother, Lakshmana.

Life in the forest among the wild animals and insects was not a picnic. Rama endured the stay in the jungle, not with anger and resentment but as a way of life. While they were deep in the forest, the demon king of Sri Lanka abducted Sita.

Rama loved his wife so much that he, along with his brother Lakshmana, began their long, arduous search for Sita. Rama and Lakshmana went all the way from North India to the Southern tip of India. They formed an army, built a bridge across the ocean between South India and Sri Lanka, and reached the island of Sri Lanka. In Sri Lanka, a lengthy battle ensued resulting in the defeat of Ravana's army and finally, Ravana's death. After rescuing Sita from the clutches of Ravana, they triumphantly returned to the mainland at the end of their fourteen years of exile. Having completed the fourteen years of exile in the forest, Rama's crowning as the Emperor took place on an auspicious occasion. Rama's rule lasted for several years. His reign was a symbol of peace, justice and prosperity. Again, another political situation arose, and in this situation, Rama exiled his beloved wife without knowing that she was pregnant.

The epic illustrates how Rama endured all that life threw at him with grace and without anger or resentment. Rama dealt with the situations he encountered as necessary, according to Dharma. In all his actions, he never departed from Dharma. Rama was an ideal son, a perfect husband, an ideal brother, an ideal friend, and an excellent Emperor. It is because of the way Rama righteously conducted his life, even under the disastrous conditions life imposed on him, the very acme of perfection, that Hindus worship Rama. There are several such messages in the *Ramayana* that are relevant to our present-day situation. Hindus consider Rama as an *avatar*, a reincarnation of Divinity, but he never proclaimed his divinity. In every respect, Rama's life is a message about how one should live while adhering to Dharma.

On the other hand, the *Mahabharata* literally means a great story. It is a story of the dynamic war that took place around 5000 years ago, between two related families, the Pandavas and the Kauravas, over a kingdom in northern India. The *Mahabharata* also contains the dialogue between Lord Krishna and the warrior-prince Arjuna, known as the *Bhagavad Gita*. In this dialogue, Krishna expounds the fundamentals of Hindu religion and Hindu Dharma lucidly.

For Hindus, Lord Krishna is an *avatar*, an incarnation of God.

There are several stories in the *Mahabharata* as well that are relevant to our present-day situations.

2.4 The Bhagavad Gita

The *Bhagavad Gita* is a unique book for all ages. Its teachings are universal and belong to all human beings and not to any religion, cult or country.

Very few Hindus would have read the *Vedas*, *Upanishads* or *Agamas*, but almost all Hindus know the basic storyline of the *Ramayana* and the *Mahabharata*. The *Bhagavad Gita* is a chapter within the *Mahabharata*, a dialogue between Lord Krishna and the Pandava prince, Arjuna, in Kurukshetra, amidst the great war between the Pandavas and the Kauravas. During this dialogue, Lord Krishna reveals the spiritual truth of Yoga, Vedanta, Bhakti and Karma to a confused and reluctant Arjuna.

Sage Vyasa later recorded Lord Krishna's teachings as the Divine Songs or the Bhagavad (given by the Lord) Gita (songs), consisting of eighteen chapters with 700 Sanskrit verses.

For present-day Hindus, the *Bhagavad Gita* represents a book that can be considered as an equivalent to other religious texts, like the Bible.

Sri Sathya Baba has described Gita as follows:

> *'Gia is the universal Mother.*
> *Gita is the messenger of Divine (God).*
> *Gita is the lifeboat to cross the ocean of life.*
> *Gita is the staff and support for spiritual seekers.*
> *Gita is a casket of sacred mantras.*
> *Gita is a beautiful garden of flowers.*
> *Gita is the royal road to liberation.'*

The ultimate purpose emphasized in all the Hindu scriptures is to attain liberation.

2.5 The *Puranas*

The *Puranas* were composed after the epics, the *Mahabharata* and the *Ramayana* and elaborate on the hymns, philosophies and rituals mentioned in the Vedas. The Puranas contain every type of knowledge from cosmology to gardening. Some of the *Puranas* deal with the characters in the epics in detail. For example, the *Bhagavata Purana* describes the life of Lord Krishna.

2.6 Summary

Although the above scriptures and epics provide the basis for the practice, unlike most religions, there is no specific structure for worship in Hinduism. No individual or prophet has founded it. There is also no authority figure or a core set of texts to follow. The other major religions are dated in a way that you can go back to the origin. But Hinduism emerges from the mist of time, and it is a synthesis of a variety of religious experiences and offers a complete view of life.

The practice of Hinduism keeps evolving with the times. The rituals, customs and beliefs have survived not only in the temples but also in millions of households. Hinduism allows freedom of thought and is not bound by a particular set of beliefs or rituals.

Hinduism is Divine centred, unlike most other religions, which are generally prophet-centred. Hinduism is based on internal principles that apply to all human beings.

> *'The three essentials of Hinduism are belief in Divinity (God), in the Vedas as a revelation, in the doctrine of karma and transmigration.'*
>
> — Swami Vivekananda

Again, the ultimate aim in Hinduism is to attain nirvana, liberation, moksha.

3

THE CONCEPT OF DIVINITY (GOD) IN HINDUISM

There is a misconception that Hindus pray to several gods. The word, God, was introduced to Hindus from outside of India. In fact, Hindus believe in a Supreme Divine whose qualities and form are represented by a multitude of deities. Hinduism is a monotheist religion. There is only one Divinity (Creator), and this Divinity resides within everyone and in everything, from inert material to living beings. Divinity is universal.

According to Hinduism, the entire universe is Divinity and envelops the whole Cosmos and transcends to infinity.

In the Upanishads, it is said: 'Divinity who is both within and without pervades the whole universe. He is moving and unmoving. He is far and near, and within all these and without all these'.

Therefore, the Hindus consider everything as manifestations of Divinity, or God, including plants, trees, the sun and moon, animals and humans, the whole of Cosmos. It is because of this concept that one sees shrines at the foot of a tree or a piece of rock in Hindu villages in India, Sri Lanka and other parts of South-East Asia.

Hindus respect all religions and believe that the realisation of Divinity is the aim of all religions. Like rivers with different names finally flowing into the ocean and emerging as one, religions may take different paths but ultimately lead to the same ocean of Divinity, God. Lord Krishna makes this clear in the *Bhagavad Gita*, chapter 7, verse 21 & 22, as follows:

> *'Whosoever desires to worship whatever deity using any name, form and method with faith. I make faith steady in that very deity. Endowed with steady faith, they worship that deity and obtain their wishes through that deity. Those wishes are indeed granted by Me.'*

In Hinduism, Divinity (God) is universal, absolute and eternal from which all things emanate and to which all return. All human beings are Divine, and all are essentially one. Everything is connected and the same Divinity resides in every human being as Atman or *Atma*, the eternal self.

The Indian sage, Ramana Maharshi, mentioned that of all the definitions of Divinity, GOD, 'None is indeed so well put as the biblical statement: *I AM THAT I AM*'.

In the *Bhagavad Gita*, chapter 10, verse 20, Krishna amplifies this concept to Arjuna as follows:

> *'I am the ultimate consciousness situated within the heart of all living entities, and I am the beginning, the middle and the end as well of all living entities.'*

According to Swami Chinmayananda:

> *'Love is the very basis of Hinduism. If you know how to Love, then you are a Hindu. All great people became great because of their love for others. They gained greatness because they learnt to love.'*

The essential texts in Hinduism provide different spiritual concepts and paths to achieve liberation but do not impose any specific path on the follower. As a result, Hinduism allows freedom of thought. No Hindu is bound to accept any particular set of beliefs or rituals. Hindus need not believe in anything. Believing is accepting an idea without any understanding. Believing in some concept is not in Hinduism. In Hinduism, it is left to the individual to reflect upon and think, investigate and inquire about the spiritual ideas and concepts provided by the scriptures, and select and accept what suits them best to achieve moksha, Enlightenment. Therein lie the glory and greatness of Hinduism. It allows diverse views and tolerates diversity, not only internally but also externally.

4

THE CONCEPT OF HINDU MURTIS

Hinduism has an ancient and extensive tradition rooted in iconography. In Hinduism, an image of the Divinity represents emotional and spiritual values. A *murti* (deity/idol) in itself is not the God it represents, but a symbol that reminds the worshipper of something emotional and of real value.

Specific Hindu deities are also referred to as Yantras. Yantras are predominantly regarded as devices for devotional practices, as an object to direct our mind and worship. Yantras are geometrical design imprints on copper or silver plates. Yantras can also be a deity in a physical geometrical form that represents the Divine power. This is why Vedic Yantras are named after Dive entities such as Ganesa -Yantra, Devi-Yantra, Gopala-Yantra, and so on. A practitioner, by meditating correctly on a specific Yantra and using particular mantras to invoke their potencies, is also able to awake higher powers within his or her mind and Consciousness. For example, Indian mathematician Srinivas Ramanujan was able to publish papers on mathematics without formal education in mathematics, which the leading lights of the day in mathematics considered outstanding. As a result, Ramanujan gained a scholarship to the University of Cambridge, England. At Cambridge University Godfrey H. Hardy, Fellow of the Royal Society was the mentor for Ramanujan, and he collaborated with Ramanujan in research and produced works in mathematics that are still valid for present-day scientific research. When Godfrey Hardy asked

Ramanujan how he got this mathematical knowledge, he replied that his Devi blessed him with mathematics. Such is the power of Devi-Yantra.

Symbolism is a part of the human vocabulary that expresses and reveals what common words cannot. Symbols add new dimensions and significance to the reality and meaning of things. When words fail to express one's thoughts, then symbols come to the rescue. For example, a chemical formula representing a substance that cannot be described adequately in words, but it has a special significance and understanding to the scientist. Similarly, symbols play an essential part in Hinduism, which recognises that all finite things are symbols of the infinite. For a Hindu worshiper, a *murti* represents certain aspects of Divinity and helps him to see abstract phenomena in concrete objects.

There is a science of making a *murti* of a Hindu deity (idol). Idols are created in a particular form with a specific material and energised in a certain way, very much like a human being. Typically, idols are made from clay, composite metals such as bronze or gold, or by carving stone or wood.

Scientists say that energy in a rock or in an animal or a human is the same, but it functions in a different way. Our Hindu ancestors understood this and used specific techniques to make idols. They made different idols in different ways and shapes with the energy points, *chakras*, in certain places to make it into a completely different possibility to suit a particular requirement of life.

The Hindu concept of Divinity is based on the idea of a trinity — Brahma, Vishnu and Siva (Mahesh), who are responsible for the creation, preservation and destruction, in that order. This idea correlates with Christianity's concept of the holy trinity: the Father, the Son and the Holy Spirit.

In Hinduism, although there's no order in the worship of idols, all worship starts with a prayer to Lord Ganesh, remover of obstacles. One can say the main Deity, in a temple, is associated with a sub Deity, similar to a ministerial setup, with a Supreme Deity surrounded by sub deities allocated with particular aspects of Divinity. In this ministerial order, goddesses like Lakshmi, Durga, Saraswathi, etc., would be considered as sub deities with particular Divinity attributed to them. For example, Lakshmi is the goddess of wealth, Durga is the warrior goddess, and Saraswathi is the goddess of knowledge.

Similarly, the followers of Shaivism or the Shaiva tradition consider Lord Siva as their Supreme deity and Ganesh and Murugan as their sub deities. In the same way, followers of Lord Krishna or the Vaishnavites consider Krishna as the Supreme God and have similar sub deities. Hindus are free to pray to any of the deities in temples dedicated to any of these Divine entities. Hindus are also free to pray to any deity whenever they wish to do so.

Note: Ceylon is now known as Sri Lanka.

In Ceylon (Sri Lanka) during the British rule, Protestant missionaries attacked the practice of idol worship and temple rituals as devilish and of no value. Arumugam Palli (1822-1879) from Jaffna, Ceylon (Sri Lanka), more commonly recognised as **Arumuga Navalar**, demonstrated to the Christians that Christianity and Jesus himself were rooted in the temple rituals of the ancient Israelites. He had received the title '*Navalar*' or 'learned' from the Siva monastery in Tanjavore, India, for his work in spiritual revivalism. Arumugam Navalar was able to prove this successfully because he studied at the Protestant Christian Jaffna Central School and became an English and Tamil teacher at the same school where Reverend Peter Percival was the principal. He had assisted Reverend Peter Percival in translating the King James Bible into Tamil.

Navalar left teaching and conducted weekly sermons in Hindu temples throughout Jaffna and South India, explaining the concept of worship in Hindu temples with reference to the *Agamas*. He also travelled to India and established Hindu schools and published Hindu religious books. He set up a printing press in Jaffna to print palm-leaf originals of ancient Tamil literature and Hindu spiritual books for use in schools. The Hindu school he established at Chidambaram in Tamil Nadu, India, in 1965, is still functioning. If not for Navalar's intervention, the conversion of Hindus to Protestant Christianity in Jaffna, Sri Lanka, would have continued unabated.

The following are some of the examples of Hindu *murtis* and what they represent.

BRAHMA

4.1 Brahma

Brahma is the creator of the universe and a member of the Hindu trinity. Brahma has four heads to represent the four Vedas and the four yugas. Brahma's mode of transport is a swan. He carries a book in one hand, symbolising the Vedas.

However, Lord Brahma should not be confused with Brahman, which refers to the Supreme Divinity within all, God.

The concept of Brahma is found mainly in the scriptures. There are only a few temples dedicated to Brahma, and he is generally not worshipped in temples and homes as extensively as the other *murtis*, such as Siva, Krishna or Ganesh.

A 2000-year-old temple dedicated to Brahma is in Pushkar, Rajasthan. Parts of this temple that had been destroyed by Muslim invaders were rebuilt in the 14th century. The only other known temples dedicated to Brahma are in Tamil Nadu and Uttar Pradesh in India. There is one in Central Java, Indonesia, but devoted to Brahma as well as Vishnu and Siva.

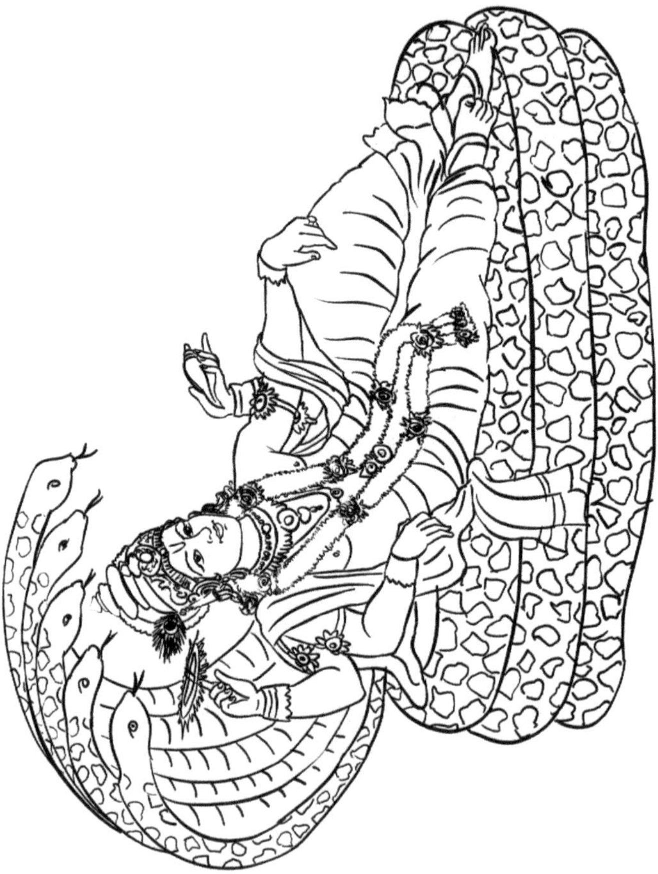

VISHNU

4.2 Vishnu

Vishnu is the second member of the Hindu holy trinity. He has taken several incarnations, the most famous ones being that of Rama and Krishna. He is also known as Narayana and Hari and is conceived as the Preserver or the Protector. In Hindu religious texts, he is described as having a dark blue complexion symbolising his cosmic dimensions and connection with rain, thunder and the earth. Garuda, the king of birds, is his vehicle.

His four hands hold *sankha* (conch), *chakra* (discus), *gada* (mace) and *padma* (lotus).

The conch symbolises the sacred sound 'OM';

Discus symbolises the cyclic nature of existence, the destruction of evil and the protection of the rightness;

Mace symbolises the power of knowledge and

Lotus symbolises beauty, harmony and self-realisation.

SIVA

4.3 Mahesh (Siva)

Mahesh (Siva) is the third god in the Hindu trinity. Mahesh is another name for Siva (Shiva). Siva means 'the auspicious one'.

He represents both the death that destroys and the reproduction that follows destruction. Siva is symbolised by a *lingam*, which emblemizes Siva's generative and creative power.

Siva is said to have three eyes, and he can see the past, present and the future with the third eye. His weapon is a three-pronged trident that represents his ability to create, destroy and regenerate. His mode of transport is the bull, Nandi.

SARASWATI

4.4 Saraswati

Saraswati is considered Brahma's consort and is revered as the goddess of knowledge, arts and speech. She is the patron of all intellectual endeavours. Those who pursue learning hold her in high reverence and seek her blessings. Her picture can be seen in schools and universities that follow the Hindu tradition.

She wears a white saree and is generally represented sitting on a white lotus flower, symbolising light, knowledge and truth.

Just like her consort, Brahma, she also uses the swan as her vehicle.

She is always seen playing the musical instrument, veena, which represents the creative arts and science.

The book she holds in one hand is the Vedas, representing divine knowledge; and the crystal mala in the other hand symbolises the power of meditation.

LAKSHMI

4.5 Lakshmi

Lakshmi is Vishnu's consort and is revered as the goddess of beauty, good fortune and prosperity.

She sits on a red lotus flower and uses the owl as her vehicle.

She is also referred to as Sri (Shri), which relates to feminine qualities such as grace, beauty, prosperity, etc.

The Hindu festival of Diwali, the festival of lights, is celebrated in November every year. The third day of Diwali, the night of *Amavasya*, holds great significance in the worship of Goddess Lakshmi, for it is believed to be the joyous day when Sri showers her blessings of prosperity on humanity. Her four hands represent the four goals in life, namely, Dharma (moral), Kama (love), Artha (wealth) and Moksha (liberation). The same way, the red lotus flower she sits on and the red saree she wears stands for beauty and wealth.

PARVATI

4.6 Parvati

Parvati is Lord Siva's consort and is literally worshipped as the other half of Siva. She is considered as the family goddess by many Hindus. She is also called Shakti, which means power — the cosmic energy that represent the dynamic force that moves the entire universe. She can change form and be both benevolent and destructive, like her spouse. She is also known as Durga, a name she acquired after killing the demon Durg. She is also worshipped as Kali in her destructive form.

As the goddess of family and love, people pray to her for her help in matters related to marriage, parenting and fertility. Women worship goddess Parvati so that they find the right partner and have a happy married life.

A lion is her mode of transport.

During the Navaratri (nine nights) festival in the month of November, people fast and offer prayers to her for her blessing.

She symbolises noble virtues, and her red saree represents purity and power.

GANESH

4.7 Lord Ganesh

The elephant-headed god is Siva and Parvati's son. He is portrayed with a potbelly, a broken tusk, and four hands. One hand holds a *pasam*, another a goad, the third holds a pot of sweet rice and the fourth one bestows blessings. Ganesh is one of the most-worshipped deities in Hinduism. He is the remover of all obstacles and is, therefore, worshipped first when visiting temples and before starting any ventures.

A *pasam* in his hand is a triple-twine weapon, which represents arrogance, illusion (Maya) and ignorance.

The goad acts as a reminder to steer the soul away from ignorance and illusions.

His elephant head stands for an unusually high intelligence and his large ears represent the power of keen hearing. The tusk represents the ability to discriminate.

There's an interesting story behind his broken tusk. According to the tale, Ganesha was assisting Sage Vyasa in writing down the story of the Mahabharata, as the sage narrated it. So, when the pen with which he was writing broke, Ganesha snapped his tusk and used it as a pen so that the writing of the story could continue without any interruption. The broken tusk symbolises sacrifice and also establishes Ganesha as the patron of the arts and letters.

MURUGAN

4.8 Lord Murugan (Skanda)

Murugan was created from six sparks that emanated from Lord Siva's third eye. These sparks were carried by the god of fire (Agni) to the river Ganges, who then took them to the pond Saranavan. In this pond, from the six sparks arose six babies. Six maidens known as Karthigai Pengal found the babies in the pond and brought them up and when all six were later handed to Parvati (Siva's consort), they fused together to form one baby. He is therefore known as Shunmugha or 'the one with six faces'.

Shanmugha's six heads symbolise the five senses and the mind that controls them.

The three essential and integral aspects of Murugan's appearance are the spear (*vel*) in his hand, his peacock mount and the rooster adorning his banner.

His *vel* signifies the power of wisdom. His mother, Parvati, gifted him this spear when he defeated the asuras in a battle.

The peacock symbolizes his destruction of the ego and the rooster proclaims the Parnava mantra, Om, loudly.

Murugan is considered as the patron god of Tamilians and so, temples dedicated to him are popular in areas where there is a significant Tamil population, say, in Tamil Nadu, Sri Lanka, Malaysia, Indonesia, Singapore, Canada, United Kingdom and Australia.

For Tamilians, Murugan stands for divine handsomeness, youthfulness, happiness and sweetness.

In Sri Lanka, Murugan is worshipped as Kataragama Deviyo (the lord of Kataragama or Kadigamam) or Kathiravel by both the Singhalese and the Tamils. The prominent Murugan temple in Sri Lanka is in Jaffna, the Nullur Kandasawamy Temple.

In Malaysia, there is the famous Sri Subramanian Batu Cave Temple with a 42.7-metre high Murugan statue placed at the entrance.

Other well-known Murugan shrines around the world are the Sydney Murugan Temple in Australia and the United Kingdom High Gate Murugan Temple.

5

THE WORSHIP OF NAVAGRAHAS (CELESTIAL BODIES)

The Navagrahas (the nine houses) are important deities in Hinduism. The Navagrahas are made of the following:

The Sun and the Moon

The five planets — Mars, Mercury, Jupiter, Venus and Saturn

And the two demon deities — Rahu and Ketu

The two demons' names are derived either from the comets or from the hostile planets of the solar system, Neptune and Pluto. These two deities are considered auspicious or inauspicious depending on their association with the other planets in one's *Kundli* or birth chart.

The Hindus accept that the Sun, the Moon and the planets influence all life on Earth, including humans. The solar system, with its precise orbits and constant motion, influences all life-forms. Even a minute variation in the configuration of the planets or the intensity of the energy of the Sun will influence life on Earth. Hinduism recognises the energy we receive from the Sun and understands that without it, there wouldn't be life on Earth.

The Navagrahas, therefore, get a prominent place, separate from other *murtis*, in Hindu temples. At the commencement of any ceremony in the temple, the first offering is to Ganesh, followed by the offerings to the Navagrahas.

Each of the nine Navagrahas is personified as per the influence it exerts. For example, the Sun (Surya), occupies the central position, wearing a golden crown and riding a chariot with seven horses that represent the seven colours of the sunlight.

The Moon is called Chandra in Sanskrit and represents the mind (mental stability), beauty and happiness.

NAVAGRAHAS

Mars is called Mangala and rules the muscular and circulatory systems in the human body.

Mercury is called Buddha and represents intelligence and communication. It rules the nervous system.

Jupiter is known as Brihaspati and symbolises knowledge, love and spirituality. It rules the kidney, liver and the arterial system.

Venus is called Shukra and symbolises love and passion.

Saturn is called Shani and is regarded as a troublesome deity whose influence in the planetary system can interfere with one's fortune. Shani stands for longevity, misery and grief. If one is under the influence of Shani, the Hindus believe fasting on Saturdays and offering donations to the poor, along with prayers, will help negate its ill effects.

Rahu and Ketu are the shadow planets, as mentioned earlier, and they can have good or adverse effects on one's path to success.

Generally, humans are not aware of the influence of the Navagrahas in their lives. However, the influence of the Moon on Earth is physically evident from the rise and fall of tides according to the cycle of the Moon. Nearly 60% of the body is water, but the brain is made of 75% water. Therefore, the Moon has a more substantial influence on our brain than the body. As a result of this, behavioural changes can be observed in people who are intellectually disabled, particularly during the days of the Full Moon and New Moon. This influence of the Moon on mental health is common knowledge.

6

THE SIGNIFICANCE OF AUM (OM)

According to Hinduism, the whole of existence begins with vibrations. Vibrations are associated with sounds. All sounds have vibrations, and all vibrations are associated with sounds. Hinduism postulates that the first thing that happened in the creation of the Cosmos is a big roaring sound. Scientists call this the Big Bang.

In Hinduism, AUM, 'OM' reflects the primordial sound associated with the creation of the Universe from nothing. This is because there was no hard matter and only darkness in the beginning. The combination of very minute atoms resulted in the generation of heat and the formation of hard matter. This action caused an explosion, the Big Bang, and the matter spread all over the Universe. The Hindus believe that the sound that emanated during the Big Bang is the Pranava Mantra or Omkara, the primordial sound.

The syllable 'OM' is described in various ways in the Vedas and the early Upanishads. These descriptions include the Atman (the soul), the infinite, the Truth, and the ultimate reality. OM (AUM) is the most sacred sound, word, and the most important symbol in Hinduism.

All the names in the world, like tree, flower, mountain, animal, are particular names referring to specific forms/ shapes. Divinity is not the name of a specific form but is a universal form. Divinity is not here or there but everywhere, and therefore, one cannot summon the Divinity by a name. A particular language of a nation cannot designate Divinity everywhere. A comprehensive language is required to refer to Divinity. But there is no inclusive language as languages are local. Realising this, the Divine Seers who lived during the Vedic period gave the Supreme Creator, Divinity, the sound **'AUM'**, which stands at the root of all languages.

'A' is the natural sound created by every creature when the throat is opened, the last letter 'M' is uttered when closing the lips, and the sound 'U' is created as one carries the sound 'A' to 'M' from the throat to the lips. These three sounds cover the whole field of articulation of sound. AUM is the universal sound given to the Divinity.

The sound AUM has been distorted by the culture and languages of different regions. For example, AUM has taken the sound OM with the influence of Sanskrit in Hinduism. In Christianity, which originated in Jerusalem, it is AMEN. But in the Vatican, it is recited as AAAAMEN. In Islam, it is recited as AMEEN.

The symbol representing the sound AUM (OM) is a part of the iconography produced in the ancient and medieval era, in the manuscripts, temples and monasteries of Buddhism, Jainism and Sikhism. OM has a spiritual meaning in all Indian Dharmas. Epigraphical variations of OM are found in many Asian countries.

Following are the examples of various scripts in which OM is written:

Sanskrit

Tamil

Chinese

Indonesian

Japanese

The symbol of AUM (OM) is also found on coins. For example, coins that date back to the 1st and 4th century CE, embossed with OM along with other symbols, have been found in Sri Lanka.

In the *Bhagavad Gita*, in chapter 8, verse 13 and chapter 17, verse 24, Krishna speaks about OM. Translations of the verses are as follows:

> *'Anyone uttering the indestructible monosyllable OM, transcendental sound vibration of the ultimate Truth, remembering Me continuously; thus, relinquishing their body in this way achieves the supreme goal.*
>
> *Therefore, in accordance to the ordinances of the Vedic scriptures, duties based on sacrifice, charity and austerity, by followers of Vedanta and the Ultimate Truth always begin well by pronouncing OM the eternal, transcendental sound vibration of the Ultimate Consciousness.'*

OM (AUM) is the predominant force of power and for this reason, as per the Vedic scriptures, the chanting of OM, a minimum of three times, before every auspicious activity is essential. It must be chanted with a high and prolonged note, and with great devotion. Chanting of this mantra creates a sensation in every part of the body. One forgets worldly thoughts and invokes their dominant inner strength. Chanting Om several times, say

3, 9, 11, 21 or even 108 times a day, will remove sadness and disappointments and make one content.

Chanting of AUM (OM) 21 times has a special significance because chanting purifies the organs, vital air, and the sheaths encasing the body.

According to Sri Sathya Sai Baba, chanting AUM (Om) 21 times has the following significance:

- Om is chanted five times for the five organs of actions, namely: vocal cords, hands, feet, anus (eliminating organ), and generative organ.
- Om is chanted five times for the organs of perceptions, namely: eyes, ears, nose, tongue and skin.
- It is chanted for another five times for vital airs of the body, namely: *Prana* (in the lungs), *Apana* (air that moves down the rectum), *Vyana* (diffused through the whole body), *Samana* (essential for digestion), and *Udana* (rises through the throat to the head).
- It is chanted another five times for the sheaths encasing the body, namely the material sheath, the sheath of the vital air, the mental-emotional sheath, the sheath of the intellect, and the sheath of bliss.
- The last OM is for the person chanting, for his personal self-realisation.

OM chanting should end with chanting Shanthi (peace) three times.

The significance of chanting AUM is for the purity of the body, mind, and spirit. It also brings about balance and stability in the body and mind. Chanting AUM 21 times daily brings about improvement in an unstable mind, improves the condition of people with weak health who often fall ill, and improves the behaviour of children who have attention disorders, among others. Studies of OM chanting by scientists (Ajay Anil Gurjor et al. 2009, BN Gangaahar et al. 2011 and Gabriel Axel 2013) conclude that chanting 'OM' cleanses the brain and promotes wellbeing.

The sound produced is critical when chanting 'OM' because the vibration of the sound OM can bring about a transformation within the chanter, leading to the awakening of inner power and strength. The syllable OM has three sounds (vibrations):

> The 'ahh' sound should come from deep within the abdomen.
> The 'ooh' sound should produce a feeling of vibration in the chest and neck.
>
> With the final 'mmm' sound, one should feel the vibration in the head and neck with the lips closed.

There is a fourth sound associated with the chanting of OM — the silence after the sound 'mmm'. At this moment of silence, there is a vibration in each person participating in the chanting, highlighting the pure consciousness of the self:

Sat Chit Anandam — I exist; I know I am bliss.

CHAPTER 7

THE CONCEPT OF CREATION

Evolution in Hinduism is an integral and natural aspect of creation. Hinduism explains the process of evolution from a broader perspective. It goes beyond what is visible to the naked eye to explain the mechanism responsible for creating not only the world but also the whole universe.

Hindus conceive of creation as an ongoing cycle of formation and destruction. Hinduism is dedicated to the idea that the cosmos itself undergoes an immense number of deaths and rebirths. The length of the evolutionary journey boggles the mind. Sri Sathya Sai Baba, Divine incarnation, (Avatha), a famous holy man of Puttaparthi, India, explains that the journey starts when life is formed as granite and then evolves from granite to vegetation, to animal, to human, to superhuman, to cosmic, and then to the divine.

According to the Hindu scriptures, the life cycle of the world is divided into four yugas (eras):

Sathya Yuga (The Golden Age), Treta Yuga (The Silver Age), Dwapara Yuga (The Copper Age), and Kali Yuga (The Iron Age or the Era of Machinery).

We are in the last Era, the Kali Yuga, which started in the year 3102 BC, at the end of the epic, Mahabharata, and it will last for 432,000 human years. Hindus believe that at the end of this Era, the present Era will come to an end, and there will be another new beginning.

Most Hindus believed in the theory of biological evolution long before Charles Darwin proposed his Theory of Evolution. According to the Hindu scriptures, one has to take several births, 8,400,000 births in total, before taking on the form of a human being. Life is a progression from the microscopic lifeform to the higher order of animals. The scriptures state that there are 3,000,000 births in plant life, 2,700,000 births in insect life, 1,400,000 as birds, 900,000 as fish and 400,000 as animals. Therefore, it is a great fortune to attain the human form through this biological evolution.

The human form is the pinnacle of evolution. Through this form, one can attain knowledge, devotion and detachment. The human body is also considered as a temple as it houses the Atman (Self). However, the *Bhagavad Gita* states that one should not develop an attachment to the body, or view it as the true Self. People who identify with the body, which includes the mind, as real remain ignorant about their spiritual nature and suffer fear and anxiety about their wellbeing and morality. A karma yogi who keeps his body and mind under control and engages his body in action without desire, offering the fruits of his action to Divinity (God), living only to perform his bodily functions, becomes liberated from the bondage of birth and death.

In the *Bhagavad Gita*, chapter 2, verse 47, states:

> *Thy right is to work only, but never with its fruits;*
> *let not the fruits of action be thy motive, nor let thy attachment be in action.*

In chapter 8, verse 5, Krishna also states, 'The one who remembers me at the moment of death, relinquishes the body and ascends and achieves my nature'.

CHAPTER 8

REVERENCES TO NATURE

Hindus have always had great respect for Mother Nature, including the sun, moon, plants and all other life-forms on earth. In the Puranas and other scriptures, great importance has been attributed to plants as they form the foundation of life. Special status has also been accorded to some plants. A few familiar plants with distinct reverence are:

Banyan tree *(Ficus India),*
Bo **tree or Peepal tree** *(Ficus Religiosa),*
Audumbar **tree** *(Ficus Racemosa),*
Banana plant *(Musa Acuminate),*
Mango tree *((Mangifera Indica)*
Coconut tree *(Cocos Nucifera), and*
Tulsi plant *(Ocimum Tenuiflorum).*

The peepal and *audumbar* trees are 24-hour oxygen generators and are very important for ecological balance. The Hindus revere these trees, and in order to protect these trees, they are associated with some of the Hindu deities.

The Bo tree (Bodhi or Peepal, Ficus *religiosa*) has a special place in Buddhism because it is believed that under the Peepal or Bo tree Prince Siddhartha meditated, attained enlightenment and became a Buddha. This Peepal tree under which Buddha meditated is in Bodh Gaya, Bihar, India. In 288 BC, Sanghamittra, the daughter of King Asoka, brought a branch of this tree to Sri Lanka and planted it in Anuradhapura.

It's been growing continually till this day. The bark and the leaves of this Peepal (Bo) are considered auspicious and used in various religious ceremonies.

Likewise, banana leaves are considered clean and pure, and food and offerings are served on it.

LEAVES OF BO TREE

The bark, wood and leaves of the mango tree are used in a variety of Hindu prayers and ceremonies.

Purna Kumbha

The Purna Kumbha (*Kumbam* in Tamil) signifies the idea that human beings are a part of nature. The human body is a piece of the five elements, water, earth, air, fire and space.

Purana Kumbam symbolically represents the Yoga path through which humans can attain Self- realisation. *Purna Kumbha* means 'a full vessel', and it is also a symbol of abundance, wisdom, immortality and the 'source of life' as mentioned in the Vedas.

The Purna Kumbha starts with a pot, which represents the human body. A thread is woven tightly several times around the pot to represent the 72,000 *nadis* in the body through which humans can awaken the dormant divine energy in the human body. The material of the pot represents the element of Fire because the pot, clay or metal is treated with fire in its process of manufacture. The pot is filled with water to represent the water element, the life-giving ability of nature. The mouth of the pot is covered with a husked coconut representing prosperity. The removal of the outer husk of the coconut represents the removal of Illusion. The inner husk represents Action, and the thick shell of the coconut represents the Ego. The husk on top of the coconut, in the form of a cone, represents the forehead of the human body. Mango leaves representing human hair decorate the sides of the coconut. Mango leaf is also associated with Kama, the god of love.

This pot is then placed on top of a banana leaf or a tray with rice, flowers and fruits placed around the pot representing the Earth element.

The items used as a part of the *Purna Kumbha* symbolise human beings' relationship with nature, and when nature thrives, human beings too flourish.

The *Purna Kumbha* is included in ceremonies in Hindu temples and during auspicious occasions by Hindus.

Placing of Purana Kumbam at the entrance of the house signifies welcome gesture.

PURNA KUMBHA

Tulsi (**Ocimum** ***tenuiflorum***) or holy basil is a sacred plant in Hindu belief and is considered as the holiest of all plant species. The Puranas say that where there is a garden of tulsi plants, that place is deemed to be sacred and the air that carries the fragrance of tulsi benefits people who come into contact with it.

This plant is associated with Lord Krishna and is offered to him during prayers and temple ceremonies.

Medicinally, the tulsi extract is excellent for mental and physical health and wellbeing. Tulsi improves the immune system and promotes vigour and vitality. It is considered to have antibacterial properties and is good for respiratory tract problems such as coughs and colds. It purifies the air.

TULSI PLANT

It is extensively used in Ayurveda. The plant is effective even if it is not consumed because even being in its proximity is enough to promote good health. If one wants to consume tulsi leaves, they should not be chewed, as the mercury in them will affect the teeth enamel. They should only be swallowed with fresh water.

According to Hindu belief, it is vital to have at least one Tulsi plant in the courtyard of the house.

The Hindus also revere all living forms, be it animals, birds, fish or insects. The reverence that Hindus accord to all lifeforms comes from the teaching that all life on earth provides emotional and physical support to human beings.

The Hindus consider the cow as the most sacred animal because it provides milk, from which a variety of foods are produced. Milk and ghee are also used in religious ceremonies. The bull, the male of the species, has helped farmers to till the land for thousands of years.

Animals and insects help humanity in a variety of ways. Worms and insects convert dead vegetable matter and animal waste into fertilizer, which in turn helps humans to grow food. Bees and moths help the flowers to pollinate and thus, produce fruits and grains. Besides, sheep provide wool, silkworms provide silk, bees provide honey and so on. From the rocks/soil to plants to insects and animals, all contribute to the smooth functioning of life on earth. Therefore, living in harmony with all lifeforms is an essential part of Hinduism. In return, animals also show their love and devotion toward humans, promoting harmony in the world.

9

PREFERENCE FOR A VEGETARIAN DIET

Diet in Hinduism is as varied as its diverse traditions. All ancient Hindu religious texts strongly recommend a vegetarian diet based on the principle of non-violence (ahimsa) against all life-forms

The Hindu scriptures also state that all of creation is a vast food chain; the cosmos is a giant food cycle.

However, the main reason for a vegetarian diet among the Hindus is the principle of non-violence towards animals. In keeping with the principle of ahimsa, the food that is offered to the deities is also vegetarian. It is the practice of Hindus to offer food to the deities and receive it back as *prasad* (*prasadam* in Tamil) or sanctified food.

The followers of Hinduism also consider a non-vegetarian diet detrimental to their spiritual development. As a consequence, many Hindus prefer a Lacto-vegetarian diet, which includes milk-based food and other non-animal derived food, excluding meat and egg. This form of vegetarian diet also assists in the harmony of food production with nature, while being respectful to other life-forms on earth.

In addition to being vegetarian, Hindus also fast on particular days of the week (days that are attributed to their favourite deities), or during a specific religious festival such as Navratri, the nine nights in November when Goddess Durga is worshipped with vigour. An essential aspect of the fast is the devotion to a particular cause. The purpose of fasting is also symbolic self-control and self-purification. Fasting also helps to remove toxins from the body, thereby aiding wellbeing of the mind and body.

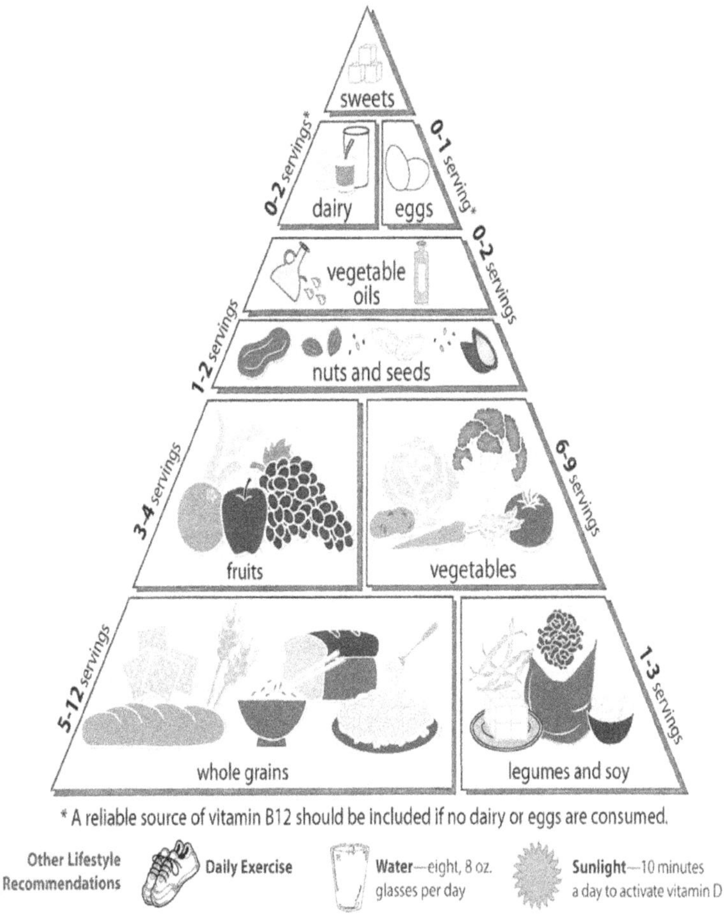

LOMA LINDA UNIVERSITY VEGETARIAN FOOD PYRAMID

According to the *Rig Veda*: 'Mankind develops the ability for progressive living through fasts that serve as initiation (Diksha)'.

The Loma Linda University's Vegetarian Food Pyramid, presented at the Third International Conference on Vegetarian Nutrition, is shown (Haddad Ella H et al.). Hindus consider egg (shown in the pyramid) as non-vegetarian.

With the influence of western civilisation, many Hindus are now non-vegetarian. Most non-vegetarian Hindus generally avoid beef, as the cow is considered a sacred animal in Hinduism. The cow is considered sacred in Hindu households because it provides milk, an important food source along with its by-products, for the Hindu family. Some non-vegetarian Hindus also revert to a vegetarian diet during certain days of the week — on the days that are devoted to their deities or during religious festivals.

Scientists such as Milton R Mills, MD and Shivam Joshi MD have found some evidence that the human anatomy is better adapted for processing plant food rather than meat. Human intestinal tracts are much longer, similar to that of herbivorous animals. The long intestinal tract gives more time to break down the plant food and absorb its nutrients. As opposed to this, carnivores have a short intestinal tract and strong stomach acid that breaks down the meat and kills harmful bacteria.

In humans, the stomach acid is weak, and therefore, there is a need to cook the meat before eating it. When too much animal protein is consumed, the body has trouble in eliminating all the waste. Dr Milton R. Mills provides some evidence of this in his article 'The Comparative Anatomy of Eating', published in 2012.

Animals also have feelings. Certain studies suggest that animals experience fear during slaughter, and this elevates their stress levels. When meat is consumed by humans, the stress hormones in the meat enter the human body. These animals' sensations, such as anger, fear, and anxiety, influence the wellbeing of humans.

It is through the food we eat that our bodies have been created. But the type of food one eats provides the kind of thoughts that come to one's mind. Sattvic food promotes purity of body and cultivates a clear, calm mind. Sattvic food include grains, nuts, fruits, dairy products and vegetables etc. Non-Sattvic food such as meat and fish promote an increase in passion, dirty thoughts etc. Eating non–Sattvic food is also against the principle of non-violence. Excessive eating tends to dull the mind.

10

PRAYERS

Worshipping Deities is a part of the Hindu way of life. For Hindus, prayer is a way of singing the glory of the Divine, and expressing their surrender and devotion to the Divinity. It is a daily routine for most followers of Hinduism.

The practice of Pooja, worshipping deities, at home remains at the heart of Hinduism. Almost every Hindu home has a small shrine with a sacred space reserved for prayers, where small images or idols of the deities are placed. Hindus are free to choose their favourite deity (*murti*) to worship. Hindus pray to several deities in a particular order. All prayers to the Divine start with the prayer to Ganesh, the remover of obstacles.

A SMALL SHRINE WITH DETIES

Besides the deities, it is customary to have a plate (*thali*) in front of the *murtis* to offer flowers, fruits and other offerings while praying. A source of light, like an oil lamp or candle or electric light, is also usually present in these pooja rooms. Some people also keep a small bell, small bowls containing holy ash, sandalwood paste or *tilak*, and incense. The offering of flowers is akin to saying that our life should be like flowers; life should blossom and be colourful, spread fragrance everywhere and be of service to others.

The pooja or prayer secession commences with the lighting of a lamp.

The oil used in the lamp represents human tendencies.

The wick symbolises the ego.

The flame, which always goes upwards, represents knowledge. Knowledge drains the oil (innate tendencies) as it burns and destroys the wick (ego).

The light from the lamp represents knowledge, which removes ignorance in the way light removes darkness. Anything can be achieved in life by acquiring knowledge.

For conducting poojas, a lamp with ghee is preferred as it attracts more *sattvik* (good qualities) vibrations than an ordinary oil lamp. When a ghee lamp is burning, the flame attacks *raja* particles in the atmosphere and the enhanced vibrations of these particles spread over a larger area. These vibrations last for a more extended period than a particle attacked by ordinary lamps, even after the flame is extinguished.

GHEE WICK LAMPS

After lighting the lamp, the deity is invited by ringing the bell and asked to accept the prayers. The sound of the bell not only invites the deities but also drives away evil spirits and keeps out irrelevant noises and comments from other worshipers.

A well-designed bell made from an alloy of different metals, including cadmium, copper, zinc and nickel will produce the long vibration of the sound 'Om'.

After lighting the lamp and ringing the bell, the prayer commences with the chanting of 'Om' a minimum of three times, followed by a prayer to Lord Ganesh.

Finally, the prayer is concluded with an *aarti*. This involves circulating a lighted lamp around the deity in a clockwise direction, normally seven times or more, accompanied by singing the praises of the same deity.

THE CAMPHOR LAMP

Aarti is an expression of many things — it could signify the removal of darkness at the end of a prayer or bhajan session, or the feeling of love and gratitude towards God, depending on the situation. The *aarti* also represents our daily activities that revolve around God. It signifies that one is peripheral to divinity and reminds us to keep our ego in check and be humble, regardless of our social status. During a prayer ceremony, the person performing the *aarti* circulates the flame finally to all that are present. The devotees cup their hands over the flame and raise them to their foreheads. This gesture signifies that the blessing has passed from the deity to the flame and then to the devotees.

The *aarti* ceremony dates back to the ancient concept of fire rituals. In Sanskrit, 'Aa' means complete and 'rti' means love, so *aarti* is 'complete love to God'. A traditional *aarti* ritual is performed with several items. *Aarti* with flowers represents the earth, water and cloth represent the water element, a fan or a yak-tail fan signify space and the precious quality of air, incense represents purified mind and intelligence, and the flame represents the fire element. The *aarti* is usually performed using lighted camphor or a ghee lamp with one, three or five wicks.

After completing the *aarti,* one applies *vibhuti*, sandalwood paste and/or *tilak* on the forehead (between the eyebrows) of the devotee. The space between the eyebrows is considered to be the location of the third eye. It is also the location of a major nerve centre. Applying *tilak* at this spot retains vitality and prevents negative energy from entering the body.

Aarti is not only limited to divinity but can be performed on all forms of life, even on inanimate objects like machines. It is performed on individuals as a mark of respect or as a welcome gesture. The *aarti* is carried out on machines as a prayer so that the object helps one to excel in its designated activity.

Vibhuti is obtained from the residue of the sacrificial fire where sandalwood, along with ghee and other herbs, are offered in worship, or it is obtained by the burning of cow dung and/or rice husk.

Sathya Sai Baba, an Avatha and an Indian guru, used to produce *vibhuti* from thin air with the wave of his hand and used to give this to his devotees to eat. *Vibhuti*, when consumed, imparts the blessing of the divine.

The direction in which we apply the *vibhuti* on the forehead (which is considered a religious symbol) also reveals the particular deity one worships. Worshipers of Lord Siva apply three horizontal lines of *vibhuti* on the forehead and devotees of Vishnu apply two vertical lines, U-shaped, on the forehead.

When one applies *vibhuti* on the forehead with three lines and a red *tilak*, as shown, it symbolises Siva–Shakti, the union of energy and the matter that creates the entire universe.

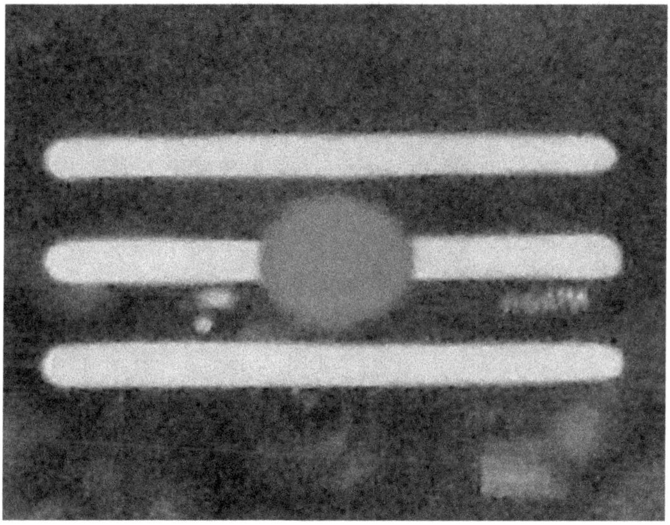

In Sanskrit, *vibhuti* means eternal, supreme, etc., and it stands for power and the divine. Applying *vibhuti* denotes the destruction of illusion by reminding us of the transient nature of all things. It also reminds us of the temporary nature of our lives — that all life eventually ends in ashes. This acts as a daily reminder of our mortality, and is an important symbol in Hinduism. This makes humans realise that we should make the best possible use of our limited time by directing our efforts at attaining liberation.

Likewise, sandalwood represents our lives, which should spread fragrance and happiness.

The turmeric–lime mixture for *tilak* has medicinal properties. It is good for the skin and helps to develop harmony within the nerves. Turmeric is also an excellent blood purifier.

11

THE AMAZING POWER OF PRAYERS

Prayer is a way of communicating one's thoughts with the Infinite Intelligence or Divine, which responds to the nature of your thoughts and needs. There is nothing that cannot be achieved with prayer. Remember that with Divine, all things are possible.

In Hinduism, prayer mainly consists of singing the glory of the Divinity. In this way, the singer surrenders to the Divinity. To pray is to surrender. It is not a way of prompting your needs to the Divinity. Once you surrender, you do not need to worry about anything and leave everything in the hands of the Divinity. It is left to the Divinity to answer your prayers in the way that is best suited to your life. The way the Divinity answers may, at times, be completely different from what you expect. For example, when you visit the doctor for the treatment of your sickness, you do not suggest to the doctor the medicine you require. It is left to the doctor to prescribe the correct medication to you. The medication prescribed by the doctor may, at times, be a surprise to you and may not be to your liking. It is only when you take this medication, whether you like it or not that your health improves.

People of all religions have faith and still believe in the miraculous power of prayer. In the Gospel of Mathew (Mathew 21:22) it says:

> *'And all things, whatsoever ye shall ask in prayer, believing, ye shall receive.'*

In the *Bhagavad Gita*, chapter 9, verses 29 & 30, Krishna highlights the importance of prayer as follows:

> *'Even if a wicked sinner worships Me with pure devotion, he should be considered a saint because he has correctly resolved that there is nothing better than devoted worship of Divinity (God).'*

In chapter 18, verse 46, Krishna again states:

> *'Through one's good deeds and prayers to Divinity, an individual finds divine contentment and salvation.'*

It is important to remember that with prayer, one can achieve anything.

Mahatma Gandhi's view on prayer was as follows:

> *'Prayer has been the saving of my life. Without it, I would have been a lunatic long ago. My autobiography will tell you that I have had my fair share of the bitterest public and private experiences. They threw me into temporary despair, but if I was able to get rid of it, it was because of prayer.'*

> *'God answers prayer in His own way, not ours. His ways are different from the ways of mortals. Hence, they are inscrutable. Prayer presupposes faith. No prayer goes in vain. Prayer is like any other action. It bears fruit whether we see it or not, and the fruit of heart prayer is far more potent than action so-called.'*

Praying in groups and singing devotional songs together is a powerful and inspiring experience for Hindus. Group prayers bring people with devotion to Divinity together. Group prayers create powerful vibrations because several minds come together for a common cause and therefore, it is often more effective than individual worship.

Bhajans are a form of group prayer. For example, at a Sai Centre bhajan session, the lead singer introduces each line of the devotional song (bhajan), which is then repeated in chorus by the rest of the group. At the end of the song, the lead singer repeats the lines from the start in an increased tempo for all to sing again. Finally, the first line of the song is sung slowly by the worshippers. A group prayer session starts with the recital of 'Om' several times — 3 or 9 usually, followed by a devotional song praising Lord Ganesh and then other songs worshipping other deities, sung by different devotees. The group prayer ends with the recitation of mantras, *aarti* and the serving of holy ash and *Prasad.* It is also customary for Hindus to clap their hand while singing devotional songs in a group. As birds fly away from the branches of trees when they hear the sound of clapping, one's ignorance also vanishes with the clapping of hands in rhythm. It is also believed that clapping physically stimulates the nerves in the palms, which in turn rouses the internal organs, improving blood circulation and breathing. A quick movement of the hands stimulates the whole body, and helps the heart, lungs and kidney to function better.

In addition to singing devotional songs, Hindus also chant mantras and meditate, as a form of prayer.

A prayer can be very simple, short or long, and is a way of expressing gratitude for everything God has blessed us with.

A Simple Prayer Could Be:

Example 1

O God,

Lead me from the unreal to real,

Lead me from darkness to light, Lead me from immorality to morality, Om – peace, peace, peace.

Example 2 (Prayer provided by Sathya Sai Baba)

O Lord, take my love and let it flow in the fullness of devotion to Thee.

O Lord, take my hands and let them work incessantly for Thee.

O Lord, take my soul and let it be merged in oneness with Thee.

O Lord, take my mind and thoughts and let them be in tune with Thee.

O Lord, take my everything and let me be an instrument for thy work.

12

MANTRAS

Mantras can be viewed as ancient power words with subtle intentions and powerful vibrations that keep us connected to the Supreme Divine, the source of everything.

The whole of existence is vibration. Where there is vibration, there is sound. Modern physicists also acknowledge that there is a fluid-like field in the entire Cosmos that connects everything. This fluid field is present even in a vacuum where material objects are not present. When we chant a mantra, the vibration that emanates propagates all around, creating a certain amount of positive influence.

The word 'mantra' in Sanskrit means the instrument of thought. The mantra could be a word, a verse or a sound (Om) recited or sung several times. For example, each one of the following mantras may be recited several times.

1. **OM, OM, OM...**
2. **OM SAI RAM, OM SAI RAM, OM SAI RAM...**
3. **OM NAMO NARAYANA, OM NAMO NARAYANA, OM NAMO NARAYANA...**
4. **HARI KRISHNA, HARI, KRISHNA, HARI KRISHNA, HARE, HARE.**
5. **HARE RAM, HARE RAM, RAM, RAM, HARE, HARE.**

6. **OM NAMOM SIVAYA, OM NAMA SIVAYA, OM NAMA SIVAYA, SIVAYA NAMOM.**
7. **The Gayatri Mantra:**

   OM **BHUR BHUVAH SUVAH,**

   TAT SAVITUR VARENYAM,

   BHARGO DEVASYA DHIMAHI, DHIYO YONAH PRACHODAYAT.

Of all the mantras, the Gayatri Mantra is considered the most powerful.

Mantras should be recited loudly because they release the energy contained in the sound and generate powerful vibrations. These vibrations dispel negative feelings amongst those present and result in the elimination of problems, worries and fears.

13

THE POWER OF MANTRAS

Hindus chant several mantras that create powerful positive vibrations through the sounds produced by the words in the mantras.

Spoken words affect us in different ways. Kind words may make us smile, a harsh word can make us angry, and as the saying goes:

The word is more powerful than the sword.

Words in the mantras are no different but what makes a mantra special is the words combined with the sounds and meaning to provide influence and effect. Mantras, when recited or sung as per the prescribed method, produce vibrations that have the power to transform people and their lives. They convey a significant meaning, and they have a definite effect.

Mantras are ancient power words with subtle intentions that keep us connected to the Divine.

Hindus usually receive their mantras from religious gurus, and then make them a part of their life. Those people who do not have a guru may select and chant any of the mantras mentioned in Chapter 10, or those that are popular and time-tested.

As a first step in establishing a *murti*, as a living symbol of Divinity, the temple priests recite special mantras. It is only after this act that the *murti* is energised and a sanctified space is created. Only after this ritual, one is allowed to offer prayers to the deity for the enhancement of one's life. Such is the power of mantras.

As a result of reciting mantras with devotion, the power of the words creates an extraordinary energy in the inner body and outer space.

There are several mantras recited by Hindus, but none is more powerful than the Gayatri Mantra, as mentioned earlier. The Gayatri Mantra, also known as the Savitri Mantra, is a highly revered mantra from the *Rigveda*.

In the *Bhagavad Gita* (Chapter 10, verse 30) it says:

> *Of the Sama–Veda hymns, I am the Brhat–Sama, also of mantras composed in poetic meter, I am Gayatri.'*

Buddha praises the Gayatri Mantra as the foremost metre (rhythmic structure).

The Hindu texts state that methodically chanting the Gayatri Mantra removes negative influences, promotes noble thoughts and creativity. It generates self-confidence and contentment amongst others and also protects one from all kind of problems.

The explanation of the Gayatri Mantra is as follows:

OM *(God)*

BHUR BHUVAH SUVHA *(Physical and heavenly spheres)*

TAT SAVITUR VARENAYAM *(THAT Adorable Supreme Being from which, all are born)*

BHARGO DEVASYA DHIMAHI *(We meditate upon the Spiritual Effulgence of THAT Adorable Supreme Divine Reality)*

DHIYO YONAH PRACHODAYAT *(May that Supreme Divine Being enlighten our intelligence.)*

Please note that although the basic translation of the Gayatri Mantra is shown alongside each line, there are several condensed versions of the meaning of the Gayatri Mantra.

Swami Vivekananda summarises the meaning of the Gayatri Mantra clearly and simply as follows:

'We meditate on the glory of the radiant Being who has produced this universe; may He enlighten our minds.'

The Gayatri Mantra is recited a minimum of three times at the end of religious ceremonies, prayers and before beginning mediation. The benefits that one derives from the Gayatri Mantra are found to increase with the number of times it is chanted per day. It is recommended that this mantra be recited in the early morning, at noon and in the evening to achieve optimum results.

Hindus have mantras for every important event.

For example:

The mantra, '*Samastah Lokah sukhino bhavantu*', maybe chanted at the end of a prayer secession.

Meaning: May all beings everywhere be happy and free, and my thoughts, words, and actions contribute in some way to happiness and freedom for all.

a) The mantra, '*Om gum Ganapataye Namah*', is chanted before commencing any significant activity, e.g., work, study, travel, etc., to provide protection and to overcome obstacles.

   I bow to the elephant-faced deity, Ganesh, remover of obstacles, with all our existence and accept all his great qualities in our being.

The Mantra SO HUM

I am that I am.

Silently repeating a mantra is a form of meditation. This form of repetition of mantras is also a common practice in Buddhism and Jainism.

Mantra *Japa* is a practice of repeating the same mantra silently for an auspicious number of times, say 9, or 108 times, assisted by a *mala* (a chain made of beads). The *mala* used for mantra chanting should consist of 108 beads and a guru (head) bead. When one completes chanting the mantra 108 times by counting the beads in the *mala*, the chain needs to be turned around so that the repetition of the mantra and counting continues without crossing the guru bead. This form of mantra meditation is usually combined with controlled breathing so that one recites the mantra simultaneously while breathing in and out. For example, while chanting the mantra, 'SO HUM', one must breathe in when chanting 'SO' and breathing out when chanting 'HUM'.

JAPA MALA

14

MEDITATION

Sri Sathya Sai Baba has defined meditation as:

> *'The correct meditation is the merging of all thoughts and feelings in God.'*

Meditation is a vehicle that carries us across the turbulent seas of our lives to the 'other shore' of self-realisation.

Our mind experiences the continuous flow of thoughts without any order or context, and does not cast away any thoughts but keeps them in the memory. One could say that meditation is a name for a period of rest we give our mind. Meditation is also a way of shutting up our thoughts. In other words, if we shut up our mind, then we may be able to listen to the Divinity.

SAI BABA

(This is a copy of a photo materialised by Sri Sathya Sai Baba in the 1960s)

In the *Bhagavad Gita*, chapter 6, verse 10, it says:

> *'One perfecting the science of uniting the individual consciences with the Ultimate Consciousness, consistently residing alone in the secluded place engaged in controlling the mind, desire less free from proprietorship, should meditate on the inner self.'*

In chapter 6, verse 16, Krishna also said:

> *'O Arjuna, the science of uniting the individual consciousness with the Ultimate Consciousness never occurs for one who eats too much or one who eats too little, nor also for one who sleeps too much or sleeps too little.'*

To practice meditation, not only does one need a healthy body but also a calm mind, sincerity, and a burning desire to rise above human imperfections.

The first area of improvement for meditation is that of the body, a cause of many addictions. Good health is maintained by a simple regimen of well-regulated diet, adequate exercise, sleep and relaxation.

Ancient seers practised meditation in different ways. They could be broadly grouped into three types.

1) **Mantra Meditation** – Chanting Vedic mantras with concentration
2) **Visual Meditation** – Meditating on a particular deity.
3) **Absorption in mind and heart** – Meditation concentrating on one's inner self.

There are also other meditation methods practised in the context of different cultures, religions and faiths.

In this day and age, one does not have the time or the patience to explore and uncover the ancient meditation techniques before choosing one and adopting it as one's own. Therefore, Sathya Sai Baba has recommended that for today's generation, there is only one right and safe meditation method — the ancient meditation technique focusing on light. Baba called this the 'Light Meditation'. Baba has also said that it is safe and effective, and Baba will be our inner guide if we call upon him.

The Light Meditation

The best time for practising light meditation is early in the morning, but it is not limited to the early hours of the day. Meditation should be avoided after a meal and preferably not within two hours of consuming any type of food. It is a good idea to practice meditation at the same time and at the same place every day.

Before starting meditation, one should take a bath to feel clean, fresh, comfortable and relaxed. Then, choose a place that is clean and quiet to avoid any distractions. The place chosen for meditation should be slightly elevated. Place a thick mat on the ground where you can sit comfortably, with your spine erect, in a half-lotus position — with your right foot placed over the left foot. If it is physically uncomfortable to sit in a crossed-legged position, then you could sit on a chair placed on a mat with your feet resting on the mat. Our ancestors used to sit on *kusha* grass mats during religious ceremonies and while meditating. The mat serves as insulation and thus, enhances and maintains the energy generated during meditation.

It is vital to hold the back, and the neck erect and still, with the right palm placed over the left palm and the thumbs touching each other (the Buddhist method). The eyes must be half or fully closed so that you are not distracted. Then, slowly try to relax the whole body starting from the neck, shoulders, hands, chest, teeth, stomach, back and legs.

In the Hindu practice, the hands are placed on the knees with the thumb and forefinger of each hand touching each other, the rest of the fingers extended and the palm open and facing upwards, as shown.

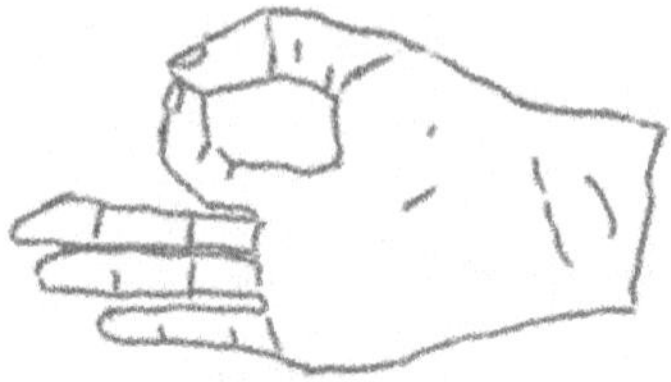

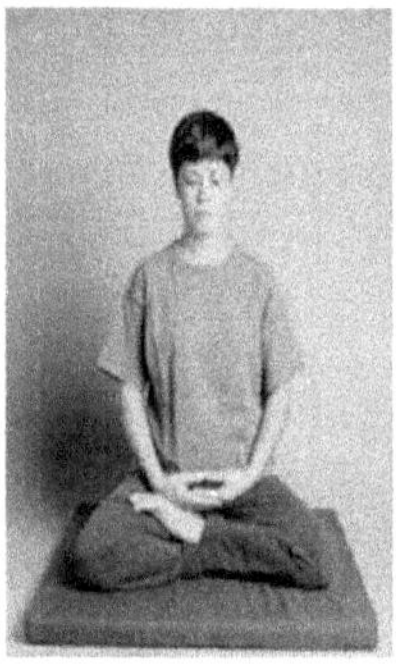

Breathe deeply, slowly and evenly for a few minutes, say three minutes, while focusing on the tip of your nose. As you inhale, mentally chant the sound 'SO' and as you exhale again mentally chant 'HUM'. One doesn't need to use the mantra 'SO-HUM' for this exercise; you can choose any other mantra you are familiar with or to suit your faith, say 'JE-SU' or 'BUD-DHO'.

Once seated comfortably, say a prayer inviting the divine to provide you with guidance. The Gayatri Mantra is a suitable mantra that can be chanted three times before commencing any meditation.

Breathe evenly with the sound of the 'SO-HUM' mantra, as mentioned above. Close the eyes and imagine that there is a light in front of you. Keep visualising this light for a few moments. Using your imagination, bring this light to the forehead, between the two eyebrows, and slowly move this light into your head and fill the whole head with this light.

Once the light fills your head, think the thought below:

'Wherever there is light, darkness cannot be present, and I will only have good thoughts.'

Those of us who are unable to visualise the light can gaze at the flame of a lamp or candle for a few minutes and then close the eyes and try and concentrate on this light. To visualise the light in this manner also requires some practice. If you still cannot visualise the light, do not worry but continue with the meditation imagining the presence of light. With practice, you should be able to visualise the light.

Now, move the light to the eyes and fill them with the divine glow and think:

> *Let me see good in all things.*

Then, move the light to the ears and fill both ears with it and think,

> *Let me hear only good things.*

From the ears, slowly move the light to your mouth and tongue and think:

> *Let me speak the truth, what is useful, necessary, and speak kindly to everyone.*

From the mouth, move the light along the neck, shoulders and arms to the hands. While moving, the light illuminates every cell of the organs to the hands. Fill both hands with this light and think:

> *Let me do only good things and serve all.*

Then move the light up the arms and down the torso to the feet, illuminating every cell of the limbs along the way. Now think:

> *Let me walk straight to the destination and to good places, and only meet and associate with good people.*

Now, bring the light up the legs, through the torso to the heart and then to the head. Let the light illuminate the head for a few minutes.

Then, imagine that the light from your heart is radiating out and it is surrounding your mother and father. They are now standing in the divine light. Now, think that they are at peace. Continue to extend this light radiating from your heart to cover your teachers, relatives, friends, and expand it further outside to include all human beings, animals, birds, insects, plants and the whole world. Now think:

> *The world is filled with light, love and peace.*

Remain immersed in this light and send it to every corner of the Universe and think:

The light is in me... I AM THE LIGHT.

Continue to breathe evenly for a few moments, mentally chanting the sound 'SO' when inhaling and 'HUM' when exhaling. Then, end the meditation with a prayer of gratitude to God. The prayer can be:

> *Samastah Lokah sukhino bhavantu (May the world be happy) You can recite this mantra thrice.*

15

YOGA

Yoga has been a part of the Hindu tradition since the early Vedic period. The word Yoga comes from the Sanskrit root 'Yuj', which means union between one's consciousness and the Universal Consciousness. Yoga is a path that takes humans to a higher dimension or higher perception of life. In this higher dimension, humans can experience oneness with the Universe.

We must understand that Life is inclusive and not exclusive as we usually perceive. This inclusiveness is experienced by our body in a small way when we breathe. We breathe the air expelled by the trees, and the trees take in the carbon dioxide that humans exhale. Even when we are seated next to a strange person, we share the air around us. Yoga means the realisation of this unity with the whole of the Cosmos. Generally, this realisation of all-inclusiveness is referred to as Enlightenment.

Karma Yoga, Bhakti Yoga, Jnana Yoga and Raja Yoga are considered as the four main types of yoga. **Karma Yoga** is a path based on selfless actions such as service to others with selfless devotion and without the thought of reward. Swami Vivekananda summarises Karma Yoga as follows:

> *'Give your hand to work and keep your mind fixed at the lotus feet of the lord. Do your duty, give up results, serve God or the self in all and follow the discipline.'*

Bhakti Yoga is a path based on devotion and divine love. It is practised through prayers, worship and rituals while submitting to God. Chanting and singing also form a significant part of the practice.

Raja Yoga is the comprehensive method of controlling the mind by turning our mental and physical energy into spiritual energy through meditation. Practising the *asanas* and *pranayama* (breath control) forms a subdivision of Raja Yoga known as Hatha Yoga.

Isha Upa (preparatory) yoga for daily practice by Sadhguru is very beneficial for beginners interested in health and wellbeing. Upa Yoga by Sadhguru is available on YouTube (Ref 20).

Jnana Yoga is a path based on knowledge and wisdom and uses the mind to inquire into its own nature. The practice of Jnana Yoga requires strong willpower and intellect and the knowledge of other yogic paths.

In the modern world, yoga has come to be associated with postures (*asanas*) of Hatha Yoga. Hatha Yoga aims to promote mental and physical health and attain mastery over the body. Hatha Yoga is achieved through proper diet, exercise, the right posture, breathing correctly, practising techniques to calm the mind and through meditation.

Yoga encompasses more than the asanas and exercises practised in the West. Hatha Yoga is a form of physical purification and training that prepares the aspirant for the higher practice called Raja Yoga.

16

KARMA

All the major religions that originated in India — Hinduism, Buddhism, Jainism and Sikhism — accept the universality of the law of cause and effect — Karma.

In Sanskrit, 'Kar' stands for the organ of action, and 'Ma' means producing or creating. Therefore, 'Karma' refers to that which is created or produced by one's physical and mental organs. Karma is action driven by intention; a deed done deliberately by body and mind; speech included. In short, any work or action, physically or mentally, produces an effect called Karma.

In the Upanishads, Karma is expressed as a principle of cause and effect based on actions. It is regarded as a fundamental law of nature that is automatic and mechanical. That is, every action must have an effect either immediately or at some time in the future. It is not something imposed by Divinity, God, and it is not interfered with.

In Hinduism, our Karma determines what we deserve and what we can assimilate. We are responsible for what we have, and we have the power to make our life. Your life is your karma (actions). During our grandparents' times, this statement was a part of day to day conversation as a way of reminding us that our life is the result of our actions, karma.

In Hinduism, karma is the force of retributive justice that compels humans to behave righteously according to dharma, the moral code of the Universe.

The concept of karma is deeply ingrained in the consciousness of Hindus and vastly influences their thinking.

Humans, in general, carry out nearly all their actions according to their tendencies. These tendencies are developed through memories they have accumulated by their past physical, mental and emotional actions, which are deeply ingrained in their subconscious mind. This means that their actions are influenced by their tendencies and are compulsive in nature and not carried out consciously. The result of such compulsive actions may or may not end in satisfactory results. The results of such actions are misunderstood in society, in their present-day situations, as a result of actions in past lives and not within their control. This understanding is not totally correct, since humans can take charge of their mental processes and physical actions consciously. In this way, their current life will be in their hands. In Hindu culture, whether a person is literate or illiterate, he honours the law of Karma and accepts that he is responsible for the present condition of his life.

Sathya Sai Baba has said that the impending consequences of an action in innumerable past lives is an enormous karmic force. He also said that our present birth came about because of that karmic force and until we become free of the entangling, the web of action and reaction, our karmic destiny will continue through aeons of time until eventually, we do get free.

Karma also encourages the right actions in Hindus, as they understand that bad past karma can be counteracted by rightful actions. According to Sathya Sai Baba, if a seed is covered with excessive soil, then it will not germinate and grow. In the same way, if we cover our bad karma sufficiently with right actions, then the effect of the bad karma will be dissolved.

It is also said in scriptures that the deeds of immoral, sinful and harmful actions can be sufficiently covered by a number of actions that lead to good results, such as a pilgrimage to holy places, acts of devotion and performing loving service to others. Thus, bad karma gets burned away and does not grow into a new round of misery.

The *Bhagavad Gita*, chapter 4, verse 19, states:

> *'He whose undertakings are all devoid of desires and selfish purposes and whose actions have been burnt by the fire of knowledge, him the wise call a sage.'*

The root cause of our suffering comes from selfish desires, and thus, the scriptures caution us against actions that are motivated by selfish desire. The scriptures further state that contact with the sense objects results in attachment. Attachment then becomes desire. From desire comes anger and out of anger comes delusion. Delusion leads to confusion of memory, which in turn leads to loss of intellect or discrimination. With the loss of intellect, man perishes. Therefore, it is crucial to perform our actions with good intentions and reason, according to the context and devoid of selfish purpose. Such actions will happen if we see things as they are, instead of classifying them as good and bad right and wrong, and so on. If one does this, then the resulting action will be devoid of personal wishes and result in what is required for the situation.

By not performing an action, one cannot avoid bad karma. For example, if we walk away from a person who is physically injured and needs help, it could result in bad karma. Therefore, one should give sufficient thought to the context of the situation before deciding to act or not. Krishna explains this to Arjuna as follows in chapter 2, verse 33, of the *Gita*:

'But if thou will not fight this righteous war, then having abandoned thine own duty and fame, thou shalt incur sin.'

To keep the whole Universe and its creation moving smoothly, everyone, including stones, plants, animals and everything else, have a part to play. Thus, the entire Universe is a workshop where everyone is allocated a task they have to perform. Whatever the task, it should be undertaken consciously by humans as an offering to the Divine, that is, without any desire of benefitting from it. Even a wise person should be engaged in activity such that they serve as an example to others. There is no single item in this Universe that is devoid of action. Everything contributes in some form or other. The main difference between humans and the rest of the Universe is that humans can act consciously, whereas plants animals and the rest act according to their nature. Most humans also act with eagerness to reap the rewards of our actions. In contrast, plants and animals go on regardless, thus keeping the cycle of creation moving smoothly.

Sri Sathya Sai Baba has also said that as long as we perform actions in order to reap the rewards, we are fully involved in and are part and parcel of that process. Therefore, we must experience the consequences of the process, whether they are positive or not. When we remove our self from the throne of the doer and let God, the rightful king, take the throne, we are at once released from the burden of kingship.

Swami Vivekananda suggested, '*work for work's sake*'. There are some, in every country, who are really the salt of the earth and work for the sake of work, without any care for reward, fame, name or even a ticket to heaven.

Krishna stresses on the above concept in the *Gita*, chapter 4, verse 23, as follows:

> *'To one who is devoid of attachment, who is liberated, whose mind is established in knowledge, who works for the sake of sacrifice (for the sake of Divinity), the whole action is dissolved.'*

Karma is summarised in the *Bhagavad Gita* as follows:

> *'Your right is to work only,*
> *But never to its fruits,*
> *Let not the fruits of action be thy motive, nor let thy attachment be to inaction.'*

Karma should not be confused with fate. In the notion of fate, one's life is pre-planned by some external, divine power and has no control over destiny. In the epic, *Mahabharata*, there is extensive debate regarding free will and destiny across different chapters. It concludes that the future is both a function of current human effort derived from free will and past human actions that set the circumstances. The *Mahabharata* also states:

> *'Happiness comes due to good actions, suffering results in evil actions, by actions all things are obtained, by inaction, nothing whatsoever is enjoyed. If one's action bore no fruits, then everything is to no avail, if the world worked from fate alone, it would be neutralized.'*

Although most Westerners, influenced by Christianity, do not accept the concept of karma, there are a number of Western phrases that have similar meanings. For example, violence begets violence; What goes around comes around; As you sow, so shall you reap; Live by the sword, die by the sword and so on. The main difference between Hinduism and Christianity is that most people consider the concept of the Judgement Day as different from karma because karma is an ongoing process that occurs on a daily basis and continues even after death. The concept of Judgement Day, in contrast, is a onetime review at the end of one's life.

Karma is also associated with rebirth or reincarnation, in which a person is reborn after death in accordance with one's actions that are carried over from the present life. Therefore, the balance effect of one's actions can be revisited upon a person in his future life.

17

REINCARNATION (REBIRTH)

The concept of rebirth or reincarnation is accepted by all Indian spiritual traditions. This concept is familiar to most people. Although most people cannot remember their past lives, there are a few who can recollect their immediate past lives and are even able to recognise certain places and former relatives. It is said that Lord Buddha was able to remember several of his past lives.

In Hinduism, the Sanskrit word that closely resembles the soul is Atma, which is the immortal essence hidden in every object created, including humans. That is, the Creator (God) within us is called Atma. When we talk about Creator, it is the Intelligence that is within us. This Intelligence is capable of converting the food we eat into this fabulous human body. In the end, this body will die but the source of creation, the Intelligence (God), Atma, never dies. Atma is eternal but takes a different body depending on the past actions or Karma (actions) of the individual being.

In the *Bhagavad Gita,* chapter 2, verse 20, defines Atma as:

> *'It is not born, nor does it die; after having been, it again ceases not to be unborn, eternal, changeless and ancient. It is not killed when the body is killed.'*

One's Karma gets imprinted and remains in that person's consciousness. Depending on the good and bad Karma, the soul (Atma) takes rebirth in higher or lower realms. This process of rebirth is a continuous cycle in which the soul is reborn over and over again, according to one's Karma. This is called *Samsara*.

In the *Bhagavad Gita*, chapter 2, verse 27, it says:

> *'For certain is death for the born, and certain is birth for the dead; therefore, over the inevitable thou should not grieve.'*

The process of death and rebirth is similar to plants in the spring, forming new buds that grow into leaves and flowers in summer, and in autumn they change colours to yellow and orange and fall away. Then, the plants become dormant in winter, and the process starts all over again the following year. Similarly, the soul enters a new body and passes through seasons of infancy, youth and old age. When the body dies, the whole process starts all over again.

In Karma, there is an accounting system, that is, whenever we do a good deed or favour to others, we get credits, and whenever we receive favours from others or do evil deeds, our points get debited. As we live our lives, we get many credits and debits, and our next life is decided depending on our balance points.

Hindu scriptures do not mention eternal heaven or hell but provide the knowledge necessary for an individual person to experience oneness with Divinity (God) — Enlightenment (Moksha).

In each birth, humans can work through their Karma, the effect of their past actions. This is achieved by the cultivation of detachment and discrimination with their daily actions. This process helps humans to do good Karma, duties, with no desire for personal gain or ego. In this manner, humans can make progress in the cycle of birth and rebirth and reach the goal of liberation (moksha). This progressive evolution carries each soul (Atma) through a long evolutionary journey until it finally merges with the Universal Consciousness. This life journey continues for several aeons from stone to plant, plant to animal, animal to human, to superhuman and to the Divine.

Humans have the ability to end this cyclical nature of life and attain Divinity in their present life on earth, thus ceasing the endless cycle of life. To achieve this, humans should look inward and not outwards at the material world. This does not mean that you cut yourself away from the material world, but your lifestyle must accommodate *sadhanas* for looking inward. There are specific scientific practices (*sadhanas*) in scriptures, and in particular in the *Yoga Sutras* and the *Bhagavad Gita* among others.

18

HINDUISM AND SCIENCE

18.1 The Hindu View of Science

Hinduism is based on the foundation of science and freedom of thought. It never persecuted scientists like in the Western world, where scientists were victimised in the name of religion. For example, the Italian scientist and physicist, Galileo (1564-1620), was convicted in 1633 for publishing his evidence supporting the Copernican theory that the Earth revolved around the Sun, which was contrary to the belief of the Roman Catholic Church that the Sun revolved around the Earth.

Hinduism never discouraged or prevented scientific thoughts, and instead, it incorporated science into the religion. The Hindu faith was never allowed to run counter to Nature's laws, which scientists are discovering through external observations and analysis. Still, scientists have not been able to fully understand the Cosmos in its entirety. However, particle physicists have deducted mathematically that the building block of matter is not particles but fluid-like substance known as quantum fields, which connect everything in the Universe, including humans (ref.). Hindus who practice yoga and reach a state in which they can experience everything around them as part of their body become yogis. Scientists have not experienced this unity but can only deduct it. Hence, the continuous experimental research into the origin of the Universe.

Veda is the body of knowledge that formed the foundation of Hinduism. In addition to the four principal Vedas (referred to in Section 1), Vedic literature also contains such works as *Ayurveda* (the science of holistic medicine), *Dhanurveda* (the military science), *Gandhara* Veda (the art of music, dance, etc.), *Arta-sastkam* (the science of government), etc.

18.2 Mathematics and Hinduism

The *Vedas* also contain mathematics, which was essential for calculations related to the movements in the solar system that were used to predict religious festivals. In fact, the number system used in the mathematical calculations by Indians were passed to the Middle East and were used by the Arabs as early as 700 A.D. This was then passed to Europe, and they called it the Arabic numbers. The change in the number system from the Roman numerals to the Indian Hindu numbers (referred to as Arabic numbers by the West) enabled the development of mathematics and science in Europe as we know it today.

The significance of the development of the number system was described by the French mathematician Pierre Simon Laplace (1749-1827) as follows:

> *'It is India that gave us the ingenious method of expressing all numbers by means of ten symbols, each symbol receiving a value of a position, as well as an absolute value; a profound and important idea which appears so simple to us now that we ignore its true merit, but its very simplicity, the great ease which it has lent to all computations, put our arithmetic in the first rank of useful inventions, and we shall appreciate the grandeur of this achievement when we remember that it escaped the genius of Archimedes and Apollonius, two of the greatest minds produced by antiquity.'*

(Quoted in *Return to Mathematical Circles*, H. Eves, Boston 1988)

Professor Edward Lorentz, mathematician, meteorologist and the father of Chaos Theory, noticed that a tiny difference in initial parameters in a complex weather system would result in entirely different behaviour. This is the reason why scientists find it very difficult to predict the weather accurately. Nature is a highly complex system, and the only prediction one can make is that she is unpredictable.

Kurt Gödel, a mathematician, proposed the Incompleteness Theorem, which states that no axiomatic system can ever prove the consistency of its own axioms and therefore remains incomplete. He also stated that no logical system will ever be able to prove everything and Truth cannot be reached by logic. Truth is singular, Truth is one, Divine (God).

Hinduism teaches that one can only experience Divinity (God), the Truth, and not find it by logical reasoning. In understanding the science of the material world, humans depend very much on logic, which is exercised through the intellect. The intellect operates from the information stored in the mind. Information is gathered continuously from birth as a result of the interaction humans have with their surroundings. Humans collect information through the five senses, from parents and teachers, and from each and every thing with which they come into contact. Knowledge obtained through the five senses is then stored in the mind as memory. Processing this memory, collected by observation through the five senses, and by logical reasoning, scientists arrive at conclusions regarding the material world. Scientists have achieved all their discoveries and inventions of the material world through this process. This process is outward-looking, focusing on the material world and not inward-looking, focusing on the Self, as the Yogi and illuminated humans practise.

According to the Hindu Yogic system, the mind is composed of four main parts. They are:

* Manas, every day conscious mind associated with the intellect.
* Chitta, the storehouse of past and present experience, memory
* Ahankara, refers to self-identify with 'I', family, religion, race, nation and so on. In the English language, it is also used along with ego.
* Buddhi, Intelligence that is not associated with the memory. It is also referred to as Pure Consciousness. It is through this Intelligence that humans turn the food they consume into a marvellous human being. The human being is the most sophisticated machine in this world. None of the machines invented by humans come anywhere near the human body. Humans can touch this Intelligence that is within them through spiritual practices such as meditation. There were, and are, several humans who have touched this Intelligence. Siddhartha Gautama Buddha is one of the well-known individuals who have achieved the realisation of this Intelligence through meditation.

In the *Gita*, chapter 12, verses 08, 09, 10 & 11, Krishna states the method by which one can experience Divinity.

In verse 08, the Yoga of meditation and contemplation is prescribed for advanced students.

In verse 09, the Yoga of constant practise of spiritual discipline is prescribed, such as rituals or deity worship.

If the above spiritual steps are difficult, verse 10 prescribes doing one's duty towards Divinity without any selfish motive. If one cannot do any of the above, then in verse 11, it says:

> *'Resorting to union with Me, renounce the fruits of all actions, at the same time practicing self– control. This is the easiest path of all paths.'*

18.3 Cosmology and Hinduism

Hinduism is dedicated to the idea of the Cosmos.

The Cosmos undergoes an immense number of cycles of repeated birth and death, from day and night to day and night of Brahma, which is 6.84 billion years. This time scale corresponds to those of the modern scientific thinking of the Cosmos.

The duration of day and night of Brahma is stated in the *Bhagavad Gita*, chapter 8, verse 17, as follows:

> *'Those who know Brahma's day which comprises the duration of four billion three hundred and twenty million years and His night also the duration of four billion and three hundred and twenty million years are knowers of day and night.'*

The cycle of birth and rebirth is also stated in the *Gita*, chapter 8, verse 16, as follows:

> *'The resident of all the worlds, O Arjuna, from Brahma's world the most evolved material planet in all the trillions of universes, downwards are subjected to the cycle of repeated birth and death; but by taking refuge in Me, O Arjuna, repeated birth ceases.'*

The elegant representation of the creation of the Universe as a cosmic cycle is a *murti*, known as the cosmic dance of Lord Siva, *Natarajah*, (*Nata*= dance, *raja*= king, the king of dance).

The dance is interpreted as the source of all movements in the Universe, the origin of the free cosmic powers, and his gracious action in liberating souls.

NATARAJAH

In the form of Natarajah, Lord Siva carries his *damaru* (drum) and *agni* (flame) in his upper hands. The sound of the *damaru* represents the sound of creation and removal of impurities.

Agni is a reminder that the newly-created universe will be utterly destroyed in billions of years, and it will burn all karma (actions).

The lower right-hand makes *abhayamudra* (a gesture that allays fears).

The front-hand pointing to the raised left foot, signifies refuge for troubled souls.

The dwarf-like figure, a demon, trampled by Siva's right foot represents illusion (or ignorance).

The whirling of the hair depicts the dynamism of the dance.

Here, it's of interest to observe that modern physics has also revealed that every subatomic particle is also in an energy dance state, in a pulsating process of creation and destruction.

Damaru, the sound of creation and Agni, the fire of destruction, represents the idea that the Cosmos itself undergoes immense and infinite cycles of deaths and rebirth.

The idea that the form of Natarajah dance represents all the movements of the Cosmos was popularised in the West by the famous scientist Carl Sagan through his show 'Cosmos'.

A two-meter-high statue of Natarajah is on permanent display, a short distance from the main building that houses the CERN, (Counseil Européen pour la Recherche Nucléaire), in France.

At CERN, scientists and engineers are probing the fundamental structure of the particles of the Universe. They are doing so using a Large Hadron Collider (LHC), which is the largest, 27km long, and most complex scientific infrastructure producing proton to proton collision close to the speed of light. On 4th July, 2012 scientists observed the presence of Higgs boson, which was first postulated nearly 55 years ago by Peter Higgs, a theoretical physicist from the University of Edinburgh. The detection of the presence of Higgs Boson particles is considered a scientific breakthrough as it provided the understanding of how matter gained mass. A boson is a particle that follows Bose-Einstein statistics. Boson was coined to commemorate the contribution by Satyendra Nath Bose, an Indian physicist from the University of Calcutta.

18.4 The Significance of the Number 108 in Hinduism

The number **108** is very auspicious in Hindu cosmology. It is the number of beads in the rosary used in meditation. The ancient Indian took this number, 108, to be the distance between the Sun and the Earth in Sun-diameter units. The distance between the Sun and the Earth, divided by the Sun's diameter, is equal to 108 (149,597,870,700km/1,392,000 km=108). The distance between Earth and the Moon is also about 108 times the diameter of the Moon. 108 is a significant number in the Solar System as it is also associated with the other planets. According to Yoga, the human body has taken this form in sync with the Solar System, and the human body will not change the present form unless there is a change in the Solar System. If humans learn to align their human body with Universal geometry, then they can experience life far beyond healthy living.

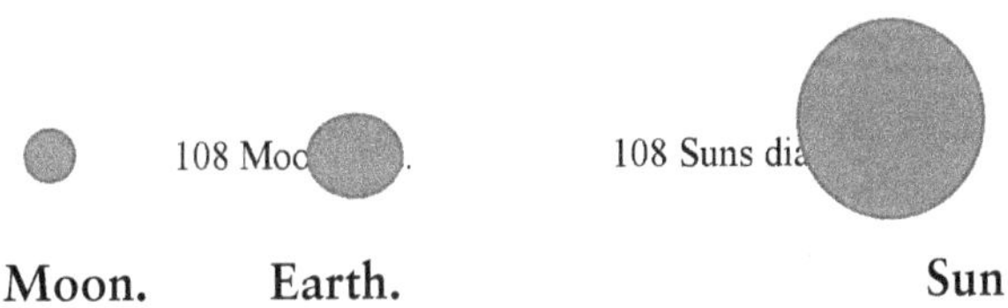

In the human body, according to the yogic system, there are 720, 000 *Nadis*. *Nadis* are the networks that channel the energy flow (*prana*) throughout the body. *Nadis* are equivalent to the nervous system, but it is more than that because it transmits *pranic* energy, which is Consciousness. There are 114 energy junction points, epicentres, and locations within these *Nadis*, and these are called *Chakras*. These junction points are similar to the junction boxes in an electrical circuit. Of these 114 *Chakras*, 108 *Chakras* are essential and the remaining six Chakars flower on their own when the 108 *Chakras* are activated. Again, the number 108 is associated with the *Chakras*. *Chakra* is a Hindu word that means 'wheel of light', named to depict the vibration of *pranic* energy and represents subtle energy centres within the human body. It is difficult to physically locate these *Chakras* because they are subtle in nature like the electric quantum field.

According to Ayurveda, the 107 *marmas* (weak spots) in the body and one in the mind are held by a chain of 108 'links'. In the inner cosmology of the human body, the number 108 is also taken to represent the 'distance' between the body of the devotee to Divine within. This is the reason why we repeat mantras 108 times, using the rosary with 108 beads, as it is a symbol of our spiritual journey towards our higher Self (the Sun) from our material self (the Earth).

18.5 Hinduism and Quantum Physics

The resident classical theory of science proposed from the time of Isaac Newton up to the mid-twenties provided a model of the world made of objects in a predictable way. These classical theories formulated by scientists like Newton, James Clerk Maxwell, Thomas Young, James Prescott Joule, John Dalton and others dealt with mechanics, electricity, heat, optics and so on, which are extensively used in engineering and technology even today. In these theories that are very familiar to us, matter is assumed to be a large aggregate of many particles, existing at a specific time and specific place, obeying the laws of motion, conservation of energy and so on. In this classical regime of science, the quantum fluctuations are sufficiently small that they can be ignored, as envisaged by the Newtonian framework, and the atomic and subatomic effects were not accommodated in the classical framework.

By the beginning of the 20th century, experimental data and inconsistency in the classical scientific theories, due to the inability to accommodate the atomic and subatomic effects, compelled physicists to accept the two revolutionary concepts of Quantum Theory and Relativity Theory. Scientists discovered that atomic and subatomic particles are discrete packets of energy. These individual units are called *quanta* (Latin for 'how much'). The French physicist, Louis de Broglie, proposed that matter and energy at the atomic and subatomic level may behave either as if it is made of wave-like or particle-like properties. These ideas led to the branch of physics called quantum mechanics.

In the theory of quantum mechanics, the subatomic particles that form the protons are called quarks and gluons. Quarks have up and down charges and are held together by gluons, as shown.

Electrons surround the nucleus in the form of a cloud, as electrons can occupy fixed, but different, orbits. An electromagnetic force holds the electrons and the tiny nucleus together.

The current understanding of the structure of the atom, the quantum view, is shown above, (Ref: Elementary Particles, Lecture, University of Oregon).

According to quantum physicists, matter in the universe has both *particle and wave-like properties.* It is not that everything behaves at times like a wave and at times like particles and vice-versa. Every object in the universe has some properties of waves and some of the particles, but it is not either. These new kinds of particles are referred to as *quantum particles* and behave like matter with energy distributed in discrete, countable chunks. That is, energy is not smooth and continuous as assumed in classical science but comes in a specific fixed amount, just like the hand of a clock that *ticks* from number to number. This idea, that some properties of objects *ticked* like a dial with a specific setting, is called *quantised*. Albert Einstein's theory showed that it is not only energy but electromagnetic radiation itself that was quantised in this manner.

Albert Einstein, along with colleagues Boris Podolsk and Nathan Rosen (EPR), published a paper in 1935, showing mathematically that at the atomic and subatomic level, under certain circumstances, quantum mechanics predict the breakdown of the locality. The *locality* is the principle that an event, which happens at one place, cannot instantaneously affect an event at another place. The paper, which predicted the breakdown of locality, concluded that if one puts a particle in a measuring device at one location, simply by doing this, it instantly influenced the other particle far away. Today, this theory is known as the EPR Paradox.

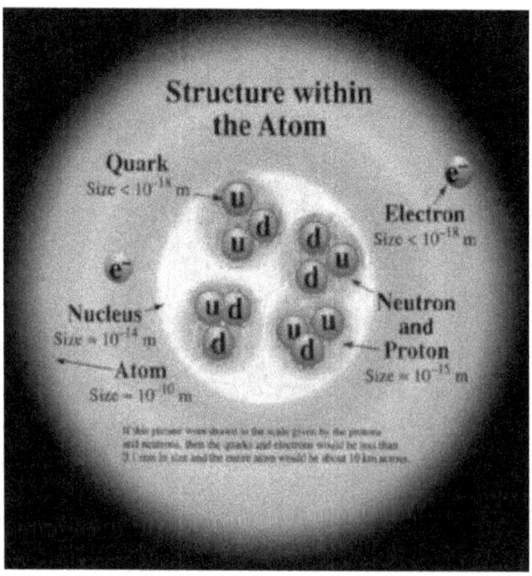

Einstein refused to believe this as it went against his Special Theory of Relativity, where the concept of the locality was necessary for him to predict that no signal could travel faster than light.

In the meantime, Werner Heisenberg, a German theoretical physicist and one of the key pioneers of quantum mechanics, proposed that the precise and simultaneous measurement of two complementary values, the position and momentum of subatomic particles, is impossible. For example, if the position of an electron is measured, its momentum cannot be measured, and any attempt to measure it will be flawed. This theory is known as the Uncertainty Principle. This prompted Albert Einstein to make his famous comment: '*God does not play dice.*'

To this, Niels Bohr, a Danish physicist and Nobel laureate who was working on the quantized model of the atom, replied: '*Not to tell God what to do.*'

Thirty years later, in 1965, John Stewart Bell, the originator of Bell's Theorem, resolved the EPR Paradox by proving mathematically that the results predicted by quantum mechanics could not be explained — which preserved locality. This is called Bell's Theorem. This theorem established that the world is non-local. Locality means no instantaneous (spooky) action at a distance. That is, a physical process occurring at one place should not have any immediate effect on a particle at another location.

This lead to one of the strangest and most important consequences of quantum mechanics —the idea of 'entanglement' — when two particles from the same source interact in a certain way, their state will depend on one another, even if they are separated. For example, if you hold one particle in Sydney and another in Colombo and measure them simultaneously, the outcome of the result in Sydney will determine the outcome of the result in Colombo and vice versa. This was proved in 1972 by experiments conducted by Professor John Clauser at Berkley, confirming Bell's Theorem. The experiments have shown that two or more electrons or protons demonstrated correlated properties even at a great distance, where no communication is possible between them, during a given time. That is, the particles can talk to each other faster than light. Bell's Theorem and its associated implications regarding the nature of the physical world remain of great interest and research to this day. Although it has been proved mathematically and experimentally, it still remains a controversy.

The above scientific theory has forced scientists to consider the idea that a purely objective world is in conflict with the theory of quantum mechanics, which reveals a profound interaction between conscious mental activity and the physical world. Although this has been proven by mathematical theory and experimentation, our logical mind, conditioned by the classical scientific theories, has great difficulty comprehending this new finding. Scientists consider this discovery in quantum mechanics as one of the most important discoveries in science.

In modern physics, the idea of the connection with consciousness has been associated with the observation of the atomic phenomena described above. In these phenomena, quantum physics has made it clear that this can only be understood as a link in a chain process, the end of which lies in the consciousness of the human observer.

In this way, scientists are becoming increasingly aware of the essential unity in all things and events.

The *Bhagavad Gita*, chapter 13, verses 15 & 16, says:

> *'And undivided, yet It exists as if divided in beings; It is known as the supporter of beings; It devours, and It generates.*

Within and without all living entities, the ultimate truth is stationary as well as mobile; an account of its being subatomic, that ultimate truth is incomprehensible and is far away yet also very near.'

Nick Herbert, an American physicist and author best known for his book *Quantum Reality*, suggests that we have merely discovered the oneness that the physical world and consciousness cannot be regarded as separate entities. He has also stated that appearance is what we see and everything around us. Reality is the secret behind things. There is a connection between them, and it is at the level of reality and not at the level of appearance. This underground connection can be proven but not seen.

Quantum physicists now say that each part of the universe contains all the information present in the entire cosmos itself, just like the tiny seed of the banyan tree contains all the information to replicate itself.

In Hinduism, Consciousness is Brahman, who is present in everything. Hinduism continually refers to the awareness of unity and mutual interaction of all things and events, just like the quantum particles affecting each other even though they are separated by vast distances. This ultimate reality, which manifests in all things where all things are parts, is called Brahman.

Hinduism arrived at the same conclusions starting from the inner realm, whereas scientists have arrived at it from the external world.

As scientists go deeper and deeper with these new theories, they keep finding that there is a fuzzy world underlying matter and material objects.

Niels Bohr proposed that a particle is whatever it is measured to be, wave or particle, but cannot be assumed to have specific properties or even to exist until it is measured.

If a scientist looks for a particle using a particle detector, then he finds a particle, but if the scientist looks for a wave and uses a wave detector, then he finds a wave pattern. In short, Bohr was saying that objective reality does not exist. As the underlying nature of the whole universe is becoming fuzzier, it appears as an illusion to the scientists.

In Hinduism, the concept of Maya explains this kind of illusion. Maya refers to that which is not — an illusion. According to Hinduism, Maya is a web of deception weaved by the universal spider, Brahman, to envelop the world in delusion. The world is both real because it exists, and unreal because it is not what it appears to be — just like the electron can be a wave or a particle.

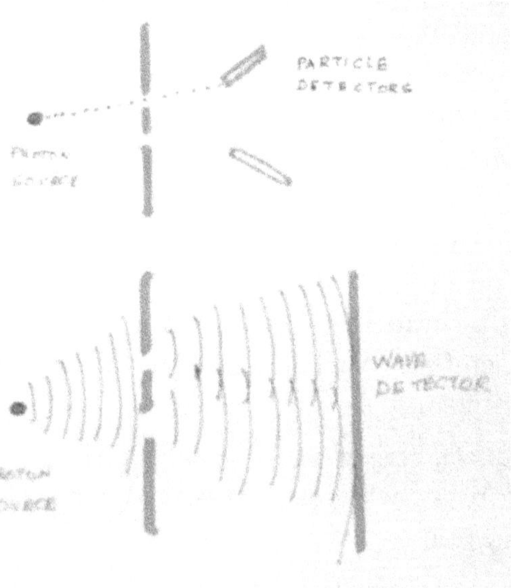

Hinduism considers the universe to be unreal in an absolute and eternal sense. The material universe is a temporary creation and keeps changing continuously, never staying the same. It is an illusion because it conceals the truth and reveals itself differently each time we perceive it.

Physical science started by explaining the mysteries of the external world, but at the farthest end of this research, the subatomic level, it finds itself face to face with the mystery of man, mind and consciousness.

Hinduism constantly refers to unity and the mutual interaction of all things and events. This ultimate reality is called Brahman, the one who pervades all things. This essential oneness is not only the central theme of Hinduism but also an important revolution in modern physics, which becomes apparent at the atomic level when scientists delve into the realm of subatomic particles.

Science has no conflict with Hinduism or religion in general. Both have the identical aim of discovering the truth and helping humans to achieve their full potential. But each by itself has only been partially successful. While the older Eastern civilization took guidance from the scriptures of Hinduism and other religions that followed, modern Western civilization took guidance from science.

The achievement of both civilizations in creating a harmonious, peaceful world has been limited. Regardless, scientists, who started from the external world, and Hinduism, which started from the inner realm, have arrived at the same conclusion of the essential oneness of the universe.

The combination of the two disciplines — science and religion — in the life of human beings will help them to grow physically, mentally and spiritually, thus building a more complete society.

Swami Vivekananda lucidly expressed the above as follows:

> *'Each soul is potentially divine. The goal is to manifest this Divinity within, by controlling nature, external and internal. Do this either by work, or worship, or psychic control, or philosophy — by one or more or all of these — and be free. This is the*

> *whole of religion. Doctrines, or dogmas, or rituals, or books, or temples, or forms, are but secondary details.'*

Ancient Hindu thinkers and rishis did not talk about religion and science as we do now. They categorised knowledge into two — *Apara Vidya* (material knowledge) and *Para Vidya* (spiritual knowledge). One is incomplete without the other.

APPENDIX A

THE GRANTHA SCRIPT

𑌕	𑌖	𑌗	𑌘	𑌙
k	kh	g	gh	ṅ
𑌚	𑌛	𑌜	𑌝	𑌞
c	ch	j	jh	ñ
𑌟	𑌠	𑌡	𑌢	𑌣
ṭ	ṭh	ḍ	ḍh	ṇ
𑌤	𑌥	𑌦	𑌧	𑌨
t	th	d	dh	n
𑌪	𑌫	𑌬	𑌭	𑌮
p	ph	b	bh	m
𑌯	𑌰	𑌲	𑌵	𑌳
y	r	l	v	ḷ
𑌶	𑌷	𑌸	𑌹	
ś	ṣ	s	h	

𑌅	𑌆	𑌇	𑌈	𑌉	𑌊
a	ā	i	ī	u	ū
𑌋	𑍠	𑌌	𑍡		
ṛ	ṝ	ḷ	ḹ		
𑌏	𑌐	𑌓	𑌔		
e	ai	o	au		
𑌂	𑌃				
ṁ	ḥ				

REFERENCES

1. Bhalla, P. P. *HINDU Rites, Rituals, Customs & Traditions*. (2009).
2. BHAGAVAD GITA TRUT. *Bhagavad Gita*. (1988-2015) USA.
3. Einstein, Albert and Plank, Max. *Quantum Mechanics for Beginners*.
4. Einstein, Albert; Podolsky, Boris; Rosan, Nathan. *Can Quantum Mechanical Description of Physical Reality Be Considered Complete?* (1935).
5. Gangaahar B N et al. *Neurohemodynamic correlates of OM Chanting, A pilot functional magnetic resonance Imaging Study. International Journal of Yoga Jan- Jun 2011*
6. Gurjar Ajay Anil, Ladhake S A, Ehakare A P. *Analysis of Acoustic of OM Chant to Study its Effect on Nervous System. International Journal of Computer Science and Network Security Vol 9 No1 2009.*
7. Haddad, Ella H; Sabate, Joan; Whitten, Crystal. *Vegetarian food guide pyramid*. (1999).
8. Hislop, S. John. *MY BABA and I*.
9. HUMAN VALUES EDUCATION FOR THE NEW AGE. Bangkok, Thailand. (1987).
10. Krishnaswami, K. R. *Agamas (Indian Tradition of Image Worship)*.
11. Lakkani, Jay. Head of Hindu Academy of Education. Director for the Hindu Council UK and a Theoretical Physicist. *Advanced Hinduism*. (2013).

12. Lakshminarasimha B. Puranic K. H. Rangarajan H. *Agamas Susama.* (2005).

13. Maheshwari Gavri (Danielle Riordan). *Basics of Hinduism,* Karan digital media.

14. Milton R Mills MD. The Comparative Anatomy of Eating. Vegsource 2009.

15. Shivam Joshi MD, Physician. 'Think we evolved to eat meat? Think again'. Huffington Post

16. Sivananda, Sri Swami. *THE BHAGAVAD GITA.* (1982).

17. Sutton, N. Professor at Oxford Centre of Hindu Studies, Continuing Education Department. (Ref www.ochs.org.uk/ced). *Talks on Hindu Religious Philosophy.* (2008-2013).

18. University of Oregon. Elementary particles.

19. Wikipedia -Used for general background information.

20. Isha Yoga by Sadhguru, 2016.

GLOSSARY

Asana:	Physical postures that prepare one to achieve union with the individual's higher nature.
Atma:	Atma is the most subtle aspect of one's being and that which is unaffected, without change and timeless and referred to as Soul in some religions.
Avatar:	Appearance or reincarnation of God on earth, for the sake of his devotees, to restore order and moral.
Bhagavan:	Lord. Supreme God-head.
Dharma:	Righteous actions based on love towards oneself and others.
Guru:	A spiritual guide. Guru literally means to dispel darkness -enlightenment.
Karma:	Action. It also refers to the reactions that a person must experience due to his/her actions.
Maya:	That power of bewilderment, which gives the appearance of reality. That which is unreal and that hinder the perception of reality.
Mantra	It is a sequence of powerful words used to achieve a result.

Moksha:	Refers to liberation, release from birth and rebirth compelled by the law of karma.
Prana:	Sanskrit word which means form breath to Universal Consciousness. It refers to fundamental life force, 'vital energy'.
Sai:	The Divine Mother of all.
Sadhana:	The spiritual practice in everyday life. Mind and heart purified by words, thoughts and actions.
Samsara:	Refers to the repetitive nature of the life cycle.
Saris:	It is a traditional costume worn by most women in the Indian subcontinent.
Upanishads:	A category of Hindu scriptures.
Vedas:	The breath of God from which knowledge is gained of the unseen and support of the seen. The literal meaning is 'Knowledge'.
Yogi (male):	A spiritual aspirant who seeks union with God Through specific mental and physical disciplines, which are known as yoga
Yogini (female):	A spiritual aspirant who seeks union with God through specific mental and physical disciplines, which are known as yoga

ABOUT THE AUTHOR

Kandiah Sivaloganathan hails from a traditional Hindu family from the village of Suthumali, Jaffna, Sri Lanka. He completed his early education in Sri Lanka, at Manipay Hindu College, Jaffna, and at St Benedict's College, Colombo. He graduated in Engineering with honours from the University of Ceylon, Sri Lanka. Thereafter, Mr. Sivaloganathan obtained his Master's degree in Engineering from the University of New South Wales, Sydney, Australia.

He still holds the membership of the Institution of Engineers, London, UK and Hong Kong. Mr. Sivaloganathan has travelled extensively and has worked both as an engineer and a consultant in Sri Lanka, United Kingdom, Hong Kong and Australia. He has authored several technical papers in civil and geotechnical engineering, and a book titled – 'A Brief Introduction to Hinduism'.

He had shown a keen interest in spirituality from his early years itself and has devoted his life to spiritual pursuits ever since. He is a devotee of Bhagawan Sri Sathya Sai Baba and has been involved with the Sathya Sai Movement for more than 35 years. He was also an active member of the Sathya Sai Centre of Hong Kong. He and his wife Jeyaranjitham and sons, Lavan and Soruban were fortunate to have interviews with Bhagawan Sri Sathya Sai Baba in 1988.

www.ingramcontent.com/pod-product-compliance
Lightning Source LLC
La Vergne TN
LVHW021132120125
800983LV00003B/432
* 9 7 8 9 3 9 0 0 1 1 5 5 1 *